CHATTANOOGA
CHOO CHOO

The Life and Times
of the World Famous

GLENN MILLER
ORCHESTRA

By Richard Grudens

Foreword by Kathryn Crosby

Website: richardgrudens.com

Published by:
Celebrity Profiles Publishing Company
Div. Edison & Kellogg
Box 344, Main Street
Stonybrook, NY 11790-0344
(631) 862-8555
Fax: (631) 862-0139
Email: celebpro4@aol.com

Edited by Madeline Grudens

Library of Congress Control Number: 2004102631

ISBN: 1-57579-277-X

Printed in the United States of America
Pine Hill Press
Sioux Falls, SD 57106

The Life and Times
of the World Famous
GLENN MILLER ORCHESTRA

By
RICHARD GRUDENS

Author of
The Best Damn Trumpet Player
The Song Stars
The Music Men
Jukebox Saturday Night
Snootie Little Cutie
Jerry Vale - A Singer's Life
Magic Moments
The Spirit of Bob Hope
Bing Crosby - Crooner of the Century
The Italian Crooners Bedside Companion

CELEBRITY PROFILES PUBLISHING
Box 344 Main Street
Stony Brook, NY 11790-0344
(631) 862-8555
www.richardgrudens.com

*This book
is dedicated
to
Joe Pardee
and
C. Camille Smith*

MOONLIGHT SERENADE
LYRIC BY
MITCHELL PARISH
MUSIC BY
GLENN MILLER
COMPOSED AND
FEATURED BY
GLENN MILLER
ROBBINS MUSIC CORPORATION
799 SEVENTH AVENUE • NEW YORK

Table of Contents

Part Three
The Musicians, Vocalists, Arrangers and Leaders Who Shared the Bandstand Speak Out

The Musicians

Glenn's Fine Arrangers

The Vocalists

The Bandleaders and Bookers

Interlude 1944-1956

The Leaders Over the Years Through 2003

Kathryn Crosby - August 2003
(Madeline Grudens photo)

FOREWORD

When Major Glenn Miller's plane disappeared between London and Paris on December 15, 1944, the world lost its premier band leader and arranger. Had he lived, he would certainly have exerted enormous influence on the development of post-war popular music.

Bing Crosby ranked Glenn Miller's orchestra at the top of all the contemporary big bands. He had worked with Glenn in their early days, and was delighted to join him in England for what, as it sadly transpired, was a final definitive performance.

In this book, Richard Grudens, our nation's outstanding musical biographer, has vouchsafed us a brilliant account of the great musician's life and untimely death, more than that, he has composed a nostalgic memoir of the twenties and thirties, which evokes that era for anyone who lived through it, and recreates it for subsequent generations.

Once again "It's Make Believe Ballroom Time," and we are devouring our triple-decker ice cream cones and banana splits, as Miller's fabulous music transports us out of our grim war-torn reality into a fabled realm of the imagination. He made a desperate situation bearable, and even occasionally enjoyable, for millions of American service men and the girls they left behind, and he richly deserves the immortality which Richard Grudens' brilliant tribute now confers.

Treasure this book. You will refer to it repeatedly to refresh your recollections of a wonderful man who served his nation heroically in very trying times.

Kathryn Crosby

Genoa, Nevada
October 2003

At The Cafe Rouge
1942

Glenn Miller and the Orchestra - 1942
(R. Grudens collection)

INTRODUCTION

On December 27, 1939, Glenn Miller and his Orchestra began their meteoric rise to the top of the music world. Americans were tuning in to the Chesterfield radio broadcasts on CBS, appropriately entitled *Moonlight Serenade*, and featured fifteen minutes of Glenn's revolutionary musical sounds that captured the imagination of America's youth with his stellar group of excellent musicians and arrangers. America had made it's decision: Glenn Miller's Orchestra was now the number one dance band in the United States.

Chesterfield Cigarettes, Liggett & Myers prize product of the day, never encountered artistic or any other differences with the mostly musical program, or its director, Glenn Miller. The Andrews Sisters, Patty, Maxene and LaVerne, three peppy Greek girls from Minneapolis, who were enjoying their own nationwide popularity, appeared with Glenn on those broadcasts. But soon the band was able to sustain the Tuesday, Wednesday, and Thursday evening radio shows entirely on their own. Many of the remote broadcasts originated directly from ballrooms and theaters all over the country, in particular, the famed Meadowbrook Ballroom in New Jersey, that has just reopened in 2003, and the prestigious Glen Island Casino in New Rochelle, New York.

Those broadcasts and band appearances lasted through September 24, 1942 when Glenn Miller disbanded to form an Army Air Force Band.

"Moonlight Serenade," of course, was Glenn's own musical gem and his eternal theme, however, on that program the very first Gold Record was created celebrating the success of Glenn's million seller "Chattanooga Choo Choo," for which this book is named.

That Gold Record tradition continues today with Platinum issues for even greater sales of popular recordings.

A record *stamper* was painted gold and an RCA Victor Records executive presented Glenn with the first Gold Record ever issued, and, on a live Chesterfield show.

In the late 1940s, I purchased an Admiral three-speed phonograph from the proceeds of an after school job in a Greenwich Village, Manhattan, hardware store. This state-of-the-art phonograph automatically lowered each suspended disc gently onto a turntable and spun them in three different speeds, 78 RPM, 33 1/3 RPM and 45 RPM. Glenn Miller's 33 1/3 LP's were just finding their way into record shops and you could still purchase 78s in album form. 45s were still very new. It was here I discovered the essence of Glenn's striking big band sounds, that special blend of clarinet lead and saxes now so familiar to us all. Not just the popular Miller repertoire, but, some lesser-known numbers: "Blue Rain," "Papa Nicolini," "My Isle of Golden Dreams," "Love, With a Capital You," and "Baby Me," the last two vocalized by a then fifteen year old Kay Starr, who substituted for an ailing Marion Hutton. I grew to love the musical arrangements and performances of the Glenn Miller Orchestra.

Well, I gradually wore out all those 78s and LPs and became a life long fan of the music that Glenn and his musicians recorded some 10-12 years earlier.

That was over sixty years ago.

Over the years, while a freelance writer for magazines, newsletters, and newspapers, I was fortunate to have interviewed many associated players and musicians: Tex Beneke, Billy May, Ray Anthony, Patty Andrews, Bobby Hackett, Johnny Mince, Johnny Best, Woody Herman, Les Brown, Wynne Miller, Connie Haines, Larry O'Brien,

Willard Alexander, Kathryn Crosby, Kay Starr, Buddy Morrow, George Simon, Harry James, Beryl Davis, and so on. Combining parts of those interviews with newly gathered material, I have converged it all into this tribute to Glenn Miller.

Glenn Miller's music is still played today and the orchestra continues to tour the world "live" fifty weeks a year, bringing the original charts to joyous fans, old and new, everywhere music is enjoyed.

In 1986, *People Magazine* ran a reader poll of the most popular bands in music. The Glenn Miller Orchestra was voted one of the top five in the nation, out-polling most rock bands. The Glenn Miller Orchestra may just play on forever.

In 2003, Glenn Miller finally received a "Grammy" for his body of music.

This book will recount the Life and Times of the World Famous Glenn Miller Orchestra through the words of many of its original musicians, vocalists, arrangers, observers, journalists, subsequent leaders, and others who shared their glory days and beyond.

American Gas Stations in 1942

*"You remember World War II.
It was in all the papers."*
—Bob Hope

PART ONE

THE SCENE
WHAT IT WAS LIKE TO BE THERE

1942

MORON'S ECSTASY $1.00

8 Flavors of Ice Cream, Approximately a Quart
8 Fruit and Nut Toppings, which Includes:

Bananas	2 Halves Melba Peach	Raspberry	Mixed Nuts
Maraschino Cherries	Tutti Frutti	Pineapple	Whipped Cream

N O T I C E : The management assumes no responsibility of any kind, shape or manner. Any person moron enough to finish a Moron's Ecstasy is eligible for membership in the "Royal Order of Morons".

THE SCENE
WHAT IT WAS LIKE TO BE THERE

The musical phenomenon, known as the Glenn Miller Orchestra, rising to great popularity among America's youth, performed in the pre-wartime, simpler era of 15 cents triple decker ice cream cones, banana splits, wartime rationing of gasoline, nylons, and sugar, all while America listened to President Roosevelt's mesmerizing and enlightening "Fireside Radio Chats."

Musically, swing era kids had legions of heroes to worship: the great and prolific voice of Bing Crosby; a young and challenging Frank Sinatra, warbling a smooth and pleading "All Or Nothing At All" with the Harry James Band; the King of Swing, Benny Goodman's swinging jazz quartet featuring Lionel Hampton's vibes, Gene Krupa's frenetic drums, and Teddy Wilson's perfect piano; the ever present Andrews Sisters, Patty, Maxene and La Verne swinging the definitive "Rum and Coca Cola;" and Jimmy Dorsey's stunning chart buster "Green Eyes," performed by his fledgling vocalists, youngsters Bob Eberly and Helen O'Connell, catapulting them all to everlasting fame.

In Brooklyn, New York, kids hitched the red and yellow trolley car on Flatbush Avenue heading to Ebbets Field to catch the action of "Dem Bums," the colorful Brooklyn Dodgers Baseball Team, and in the Bronx Joltin' Joe DiMaggio drew them to Yankee Stadium. Trolleys and buses transported many of that generation to dance pavilions located at the edge of most American small towns where the traveling territory bands and visiting big city bands performed. The depression was fading, America was fully embroiled in World War II, our serviceman beating back advancing Axis armies, ironically transforming economic hard days into economically improved times.

At industrialist Henry Ford's giant Willow Run plant, he established the mile-long mass production assembly line that turned out thousands of Jeeps and B-24 Bombers that helped shorten the war. Everyday citizens grew their own fruits and vegetables in backyard Victory Gardens. Mickey Rooney and Judy Garland tapped and sang their way through all those black and white MGM musicals. Elizabeth Taylor became a budding actress in the MGM stable of stars, and Norma Jean Baker had not yet been transformed into Marilyn Monroe. The song, "The Last Time I Saw Paris," drowned juke boxes in tears, and Freddy Martin's musicians were singing and playing "The Hut Sut Song." Prolific bandleader and composer Duke Ellington scored high with vocalist Herb Jeffries' rendition of "Flamingo." Over NBC's radio airwaves, Kate Smith delivered a hearty "God Bless America," written by Irving Berlin, and still played during the seventh inning stretch at Yankee Stadium today. Bing Crosby introduced yet another Irving Berlin immortal composition, entitled "White Christmas," which remains the biggest selling single recording in history.

Kids took off in their dad's cast-off Model A's. The average pay for workers wasn't much more than $20.00 a week. Aspirations of wealth was to earn $10,000 a year. If you wanted lottery winnings, you had to buy hard-to-find official Irish Sweepstakes tickets. Refrigerators were not yet a common appliance. Most of us owned iceboxes, requiring us to purchase a ten cents block of ice once a week or so, from a local icehouse. In winter, perishables were simply placed in sheet metal, sliding door window boxes. Babies were handily delivered in hospitals for $25.00-50.00 that included a week's stay. Doctors charged about the same and included before and after care, and even made house calls. A bottle of Coca Cola was less than five cents

On the radio, after school, you heard "Jack Armstrong, the All-American Boy." On Sunday nights at seven, Jack Benny and Eddie "Rochester" Anderson sold Jell-O between jokes and skits. Radio comedians Fred Allen, Amos & Andy, Abbott & Costello, George Burns and Gracie Allen, Bob Hope, Baby Snooks and Daddy, wooden and witty Charlie McCarthy, with his maker and voice, Edgar Bergen, entertained prolifically on evening radio network programs. An immensely popular singer, Bing Crosby, hawked Kraft's

Velveeta cheese on a hot, yet casual radio show that featured not only his top hits, but top show business acts appearing with him while fifty million listeners tuned in each week. Al Jolson was a regular guest.

The in-person appearances of the big name bands were combined with newly released films in the great first run movie houses on Broadway in New York: The Capital, the Strand, the Paramount, the Roxy, and the vast cavern of Radio City Music Hall, and similarly as well in other big cities across the land. Precisely as the film credits rolled to a close, a massive stage slowly rose to an elevated level creating a vast platform as the familiar, signature theme of the featured band lifted up fresh and bright. Exciting live music claimed you. You had to be there!

Some kids would sleep through the movie just to await the return of their favorite band performers for a second and even third show. For them, it was an all day affair. Kids would file into rest rooms to sneak-smoke an Old Gold, Chesterfield, Raleigh (with the attached free coupon in the pack), Camel, or Lucky Strike cigarette. Cigarette manu-facturers claims told you how *good* their cigarettes were: Some contained "Apple Honey," some declared that "They Satisfy." Some, they insisted, helped digestion. The tag line L.S.M.F.T. (Lucky Strike Means Fine Tobacco) alternately Jack Benny's radio show sponsor suggested "So why not smoke a few, Jack Benny does!"

At the corner candy store, only if you could not afford a full pack, you purchased "loosies," single cigarettes for a penny each with a free book of matches, perhaps while you downed a five cent bottle of Mission Orange soda. They didn't know much about the dangers of cigarette smoking then.

In New York, on famed 52nd Street, the music institu-tions were kept busy: The Onyx Club, the Famous Door, and Ryan's and Kelly's Stables, to name a few, were mostly converted old brownstone town houses for the presence of music groups, bands and vocalists, on that famous "Swing Street." There, all the great musicians played and budding musicians witnessed in awe. In Hollywood, at the Palladium, considered then to be the largest ballroom in the world, swing bands played to 6,500 dancers at a time on its 12,500 square feet of dance floor.

At the glamorous Glen Island Casino, situated on a small island in New Rochelle, New York, minutes above Manhattan, the big bands flourished in a romantic setting. Along a Cedar Grove, New Jersey, highway, Frank Dailey's Meadowbrook, another very popular dance emporium, stood ready each night where the big bands had their way with large crowds of college students and swing enthusiasts on the massive dance floor, especially on Saturday afternoon. The bands: Glen Gray's Casa Loma Orchestra, Charlie Spivak, Woody Herman, Claude Thornhill, and Tommy and Jimmy Dorsey, as well as Glenn Miller, performed where network radio remotes broadcast their great, new music to the entire country for the first time.

Glenn Miller's Orchestra helped lead that generation. His lyrically stated, exacting, perfectly performed music charts, predicated principally on his own fine arrangements and those of his fine organization, wove a fine pattern of quality popular music that captured the imagination of wartime America, whose legacy would endure and persist into the 21st Century.

This story charts the past and present of the musical phenomenon known to the world as the Glenn Miller Orchestra.

Announcer Paul Douglas Live from the Hotel Pennsylvania in New York City

"Ladies and Gentlemen, may I introduce Glenn Miller, bandleader, arranger, leading exponent of the swing trombone, direct from the Cafe Rouge in the Hotel Pennsylvania. Now, here's Glenn Miller's music."

Presentation of the
First Gold Record

"Chattanooga
Choo Choo"

February 10, 1942

Awarded on
Nationwide Radio

*Glenn Miller is honored with the symbolic
Gold Record Award, the very first such award.*

Announcer Paul Douglas: "Glenn, I would like to present Mr. W. Wallace Early, the Manager of Record Sales for Victor and Bluebird Records."

"Thanks, Paul, it's a pleasure to be here tonight. And speaking for R.C.A. Victor, we're mighty proud of that 'Chattanooga Choo Choo' and the man who made the record, Glenn Miller. You see, it's been a long time, fifteen years in fact, that any record sold a million copies. And 'Chattanooga Choo Choo' certainly put on steam and breezed right through that million mark by over 200,000 copies. And we decided that Glenn should get a trophy. The best one we could think of was a gold record of 'Chattanooga.'

"And now Glenn, it's yours, with the best wishes of R.C.A. Victor Bluebird Records," (to wild applause).

Glenn: "Thank you, Wally, that's really a wonderful present."

Chattanooga Choo Choo

Mack Gordon & Harry Warren

Pardon me boy
Is that the Chattanooga Choo Choo
Track twenty-nine
Boy you can gimme a shine
I can afford to board a Chattanooga Choo Choo
I've got my fare
And just a trifle to spare
You leave the Pennsylvania station
'Bout a quarter to four
Read a magazine
And then you're in Baltimore
Dinner in the diner
Nothing can be finer,
Than to have your ham'n eggs in Carolina
When you hear the whistle blowin'
Eight to the bar
Then you know that Tennessee
Is not very far
Shovel all the coal in,
Got to keep it rollin'
Woo, Woo, Chattanooga there you are
There's gonna be
A certain party at the station
Satin and lace,
I used to call funny face
She's gonna cry
Until I tell her that I'll never roam
So Chattanooga Choo Choo
Won't you choo-choo me home

The First Gold Record

Announcer Paul Douglas, W. Wallace Early of Bluebird Records, awards Glenn Miller the First Gold Record for *Chattanooga Choo Choo*

Paul: "I think everyone listening on the radio should know, Glenn, it is actually a recording of 'Chattanooga Choo Choo,' but it's in gold—solid gold, that is really fine."

Glenn: "That's right, Paul. And now for the boys in the band and for the whole gang, thanks a million, two hundred thousand."

Paul: "That's nicely put, Glenn, and our sponsors are mighty proud of that record, too. So now, suppose we enjoy you and the boys playing what's on that gold record."

The orchestra swings into "Chattanooga Choo Choo."

Featured in the film Sun Valley Serenade *in 1941 "Chattanooga Choo Choo" was nominated for an Oscar for "Best Song of the year. "*

DOWNBEAT AWARD

Paul Douglas announces The Glenn Miller Band winning the Downbeat Poll *as the best band in the land on February 4, 1940.*

"Speaking of being busy, Glenn has his Chesterfield Series off to a good start. He's opening at the Pennsylvania Hotel tonight and now Mr. Dave Dexter, Associate Editor of *Downbeat Magazine*, the musician's rule book, is here with something of interest for all Glenn Miller fans."

Mr. Dexter: "Thank you Paul Douglas, and it really is a pleasure to announce that America's musicians voting in Downbeat have elected Glenn Miller's band the All Around Favorite Dance Band of the Nation. So Glenn, on behalf of the musicians who took part, here is the Golden Trophy, symbolic we feel, of your superiority in the band field."

Glenn: "Thank you Dave. I guess the best way to say thanks is by playing a tune the folks seem to like the most 'In The Mood.'"

Wynne Miller
(courtesy Wynne Miller)

Glenn's Niece

WYNNE MILLER

When I first talked with the lovely Wynne Miller, I was unaware of her extraordinary enthusiasm for her famous uncle, Glenn Miller. Here, she shares her very personal thoughts about him as a very young niece and the daughter of Glenn's brother, Deane Miller. A sophisticated singer in her own right, Wynne has enjoyed an exciting career on the Broadway stage, including her role as Daisy Mae in *L'il Abner,* and has enjoyed many other notable roles: Carrie in *Carousel,* Sarah in *Guys and Dolls,* Maria in *Sound of Music,* Guenevere in *Camelot,* Kate in *Kiss Me Kate,* and Marion, the librarian, in *Music Man.* She also appeared in the films *Annie* and *The Way We Were.* Wynne Miller has developed a legacy of her own. She has proved her allegiance as in her "Wynne Miller sings Glenn Miller," album.

"As a young child, I remember the wonderful feeling I had knowing my Uncle Glenn was a part of my life. As time passes, that feeling has deepened, as I have come to appreciate this extraordinary man who has evolved as an American legend, known all over the world through his great music and devotion to his country during World War II when he unselfishly organized the greatest musical organization of his time and brought its music directly to our fighting men overseas, thereby inadvertently, forfeiting his precious life.

"My father, Deane Miller, was Glenn's older brother. Excitement always persisted in the musical Miller household, especially when Glenn would visit the homestead in Colorado to join with the family. They were great family minded people, and now he was a world famous entertainer, and their occasional visits signaled wonderful times for all of us.

"In their early years, the three Miller brothers, Deane, Glenn, and Herb, would disappear to the 'woodshed,' their name for a practice spot out back where they would 'jam' for hours on end—my father and Herb on trumpet, and Glenn, of course, on trombone. Over the years, Glenn's visits, and his concern for the family's welfare, never ceased. Glenn's father died relatively young, resulting in Glenn attending unselfishly to his mother's welfare through to the end of her life.

"I was the first grandchild in the family, and an only child. I was blessed with lots of attention. Special packages were delivered to me from the FAO Schwarz toy store in New York. Lots of salt water taffy arrived from Atlantic City, New Jersey, whenever Glenn played the famous Steel Pier. And, I loved my wonderful red leather jacket he sent, which I wore on my first day at school. Christmastime brought gifts from Uncle Glenn, insuring that every Christmas was richly enjoyed.

"Of course, listening to Glenn's radio broadcasts was a daily ritual at our house. It was so nice to hear those broadcasts from exotic places like the Panther Room of the Hotel Sherman in Chicago, and the Palladium in Los Angeles. When I was supposed to be studying in my room, I was listening to Uncle Glenn's famous orchestra. And, what a thrill to be in Kimbrel's Music Store in downtown Greeley, Colorado, my hometown, when Glenn's records and sheet music appeared with his photo on the cover. Perhaps, the greatest thrill of all was going to the Sterling Theater to see my Uncle Glenn in the movie *Sun Valley Serenade*, with great stars Sonja Henie, Milton Berle, and heart- throb John Payne. The movie, with such beautiful scenery and skiing scenes, that was filmed on location in Sun Valley, Idaho, still plays twenty-four hours a day in every room in the Sun Valley Lodge. The band was superb, and Glenn received such excellent notices. However, those halcyon days came to an abrupt end when World War II began. All too suddenly, we learned that Glenn, who was at the height of his success, had enlisted because he wanted to make a contribution to the war effort. His way was to entertain the service men and women who had recently been the very same youngsters who crowded his bandstand to hear and dance to the great Miller tunes. The next thing we knew, Glenn was back in Colorado visiting the family in a crisp Army Air Corps uniform. So, for me, it was now Captain Glenn Miller, and not just Uncle Glenn.

"The Air Force band that he created was the greatest musical organization of its kind. They went to England where vast numbers of troops were preparing for "D" Day. The tireless effort that Glenn accomplished there led General Jimmy Doolittle to say, 'Captain Glenn Miller, next to a letter from home, your organization is the greatest morale builder." The dark December day I have marked in my memory, was when we heard that Glenn was missing. I remember vividly my father lying on the couch in disbelief. He had had a psychic experience that Glenn was calling out to him for help and he could do nothing to help him.

"It was to be fifty years later when the Army Air Force marked the anniversary of his passing by holding a memorial for Glenn at Arlington National Cemetery in Washington, officiated by the Comanding General of the United States Air Force.

"Following the ceremony, a grand concert was performed in his honor by the Air Force Orchestra at Constitution Hall. It was an event worthy of my Uncle Glenn. Glenn's sister, who is my Aunt Irene, felt very much as I did.

"I know my uncle Glenn would have approved.

"It's an honor to be a part of the great Glenn Miller legacy, and, in my own humble way, I will continue to carry on the Glenn Miller music tradition with my own performances of his music.

"I salute you, Major Glenn Miller, but you are still Uncle Glenn to me."

IN THE MOOD

Words by
ANDY RAZAF

Music by
JOE GARLAND

Introduced by
GLENN MILLER

Shapiro,
Bernstein & Co.
MUSIC PUBLISHERS
R.K.O. Radio City Music Hall Building
1270 Sixth Avenue
New York

PART TWO

THE GLENN MILLER STORY

Glenn's Early Life
The Road to Greatness

Glenn Miller's early life had never signaled his future success as a true major musical legend. Inauspiciously, Alton Glenn Miller was born in the heartland of this great country in Clarinda, a small town in Southwest Iowa, from which the family moved, when he was five.

Glenn Miller's Birthplace in Clarinda
(courtesy Glenn Miller Birthplace Society)

The year was 1904, one year following the birth of two other show business icons, whose lives paralleled his own, a couple of performers named Bing Crosby and Bob Hope. Bing was born in Tacoma, Washington, and Bob in Eltham, England.

Young Glenn (Middle)
(courtesy Glenn Miller Birthplace Society)

Mother Mattie Lou Miller named her newborn Alton Glenn Miller, Alton being the first name of a presidential candidate whose main claim to fame was that he lost an election that year to Teddy Roosevelt. Alton, forever after, used his middle name, Glenn.

Glenn's dad, a homesteader, carpenter and railroad worker, lived for a time with his family in a simple sod hut and worked nearby. Like a true homesteader his mom worked hard, but nevertheless nourished her children with education, music and religious training. Glenn, a serious lad, always pitched in to aid the family's welfare during financially difficult times.

When the family moved to North Platte, Iowa, living in that sod house, Glenn's dad acquired a mandolin for him and a cornet for his brother, Deane, who later became a dentist. A third brother, John Herbert Miller, appeared in 1913, and a few years later a sister, named Irene, was born. Glenn's mother's influence on the family was puritanical in nature, fostering hard work, a demand for perfection, coupled with instituting stubborn inhibitions that masked feelings in personal relationships that Glenn carried on into his adulthood, creating higher than normal standards which later would govern his philosophy on life and business. Another move, this time to Grant City, Missouri, where Glenn sang in the choir and decided to trade the mandolin for a horn, which, some said, he played while working the "beet drys," never tiring, always playing, and extremely self-disciplined. His brother, Deane, joined the town-sponsored band. Glenn followed his lead when given a trombone by a local butcher, for whom he worked as an errand boy, so he could play alongside his brother. An active, sports minded kid, Glenn enjoyed playing baseball and football, and, at one time, yearned for a professional player's life, but feared that damaging his lip would interrupt his passion of playing trombone.

The Miller family moved once again. This time to Fort Morgan, Colorado, where Glenn attended high school and worked diligently at many odd jobs, played football and blew his beloved trombone in the school band. Before collecting a high school diploma in 1921, Glenn already had hit the road after trying out for a spot in a territory band. Consequently, in his absence, mother Miller accepted her son's certificate. Some one-and-a-half years later Glenn attended the University of Colorado for three semesters, and, at the same time garnered his first trombone-playing professional job performing with Boyd Senter's band, followed by a spot in the eight piece band of Holly Moyer, a fellow student. It

With Holly Moyer, in 1924
(R. Grudens collection)

was here, where brother Deane played cornet, that Glenn experimented with the art of arranging.

In Jimmy Joy's collegiate band there was a banjo player named Smith Ballew, who became a singer and bandleader. When Glenn tried out for the Smith Ballew band, he didn't get the job, so he went back to Boulder, Colorado, to continue his education, but soon dropped out to concentrate on his ultimate goal of becoming a full time musician. He continued working in the Moyer band, later touring with the eleven-piece Tommy Watkins band in 1924, eventually traveling south to Mexico, then finding his way to the musicians Big Apple, the City of Los Angeles.

Like Bing Crosby and other, early budding musicians and singers before him, Glenn was influenced by listening to phonograph records of popular bands; the Cotton Pickers, the Melody Makers, the Syncopating Five, and the Scranton Sirens, picking up musical tricks and ideas.

In Los Angeles, Glenn spent brief periods with Max Fisher and Georgie Stoll.

In 1925, at the Forum Theater in Los Angeles, Glenn received a break, playing trombone and writing arrangements in the great jazz band of the prolific, jazz-oriented, Ben Pollack, a musician originally from Chicago. Pollack was influenced by Louis Armstrong and famed cornetist Leon "Bix" Beiderbecke, who were performing the revolutionary arrangements of the great Bill Challis. Thanks to Pollack's solid performances and excellent drumming skills, and adding Glenn's fine, disciplined arrangements, the band reflected a jazz feeling generally unknown among white bands at the time. Among Pollack's players were tenor saxophone player Bud Freeman, trombonist Jack Teagarden, clarinetist Benny Goodman, and trumpeters Harry James and Jimmy McPartland. Glenn was 21 and Benny Goodman was but 16. The two musicians established a friendship that lasted a lifetime, always praising one another, publicly and privately.

"I've always admired Glenn, especially as a leader, arranger and trombonist. All us musicians admired him, as well, considering him to be a very generous and concerned man of many qualities," Benny Goodman told me in a 1982 interview.

Over a period from 1928 through 1931 Glenn joins in many record sessions with the Dorsey Brothers in New York, and works with Loring "Red" Nichols and his Five Pennies on most of their record dates. He played in Broadway pit bands, also cutting twenty-two record sides with his new friend Benny Goodman. Among the recordings, there were arrangements that included works by Jack Teagarden, his trombone playing contemporary and sometime mentor and playing rival. There after, the Depression adversely affected studio work for many musicians, so Glenn turned to helping others, including his efforts on behalf of Smith Ballew, who was reforming his own band. Glenn became the band's trombonist, arranger, and rehearsal director. This ended in the fall of 1933, although he remained on as band manager for a while.

Glenn and Helen

The Boulder, Colorado newspaper article ran a photo of Helen Burger, with the announcement of her marriage to Glenn Miller:

"October 9—Miss Helen Burger, graduate of the University of Colorado and member of the Pi Beta Phi Sorority, was married at New York City Saturday to Glenn Miller, also a former university student and now the highest paid trombone player in the United States. They will live in New York. Miller's parents reside at Fort Morgan. Mrs. Miller is the daughter of County Clerk and Mrs. Fred W. Burger of Boulder County."

So it was that Glenn and Helen married at last. Their love and relationship was enduring, better, it was said, than almost any musician in the business. They were truly in love and happy. Helen realized the moods of her husband and resolved tensions before they surfaced. A diplomatic and warm personality prevailed in Helen, which was the opposite of Glenn's that was rather cool and aloof to most people.

"The greatest thing that happened to Glenn Miller was Helen Miller," according to one of Glenn's best friends.

Helen was a small, quiet, and well reserved girl. Glenn and Helen had gone together when they were at the university, although it was never clear there would be a future marriage. Glenn's traveling with his music was the obvious culprit in the fact they never got

together permanently. Once Glenn realized that his life would be spent without the girl he loved, and now certain he would be able to support her now that his career was ascending, he wired her to come promptly to New York so they could be married. When she arrived, Glenn invoked his usual commanding approach and they were married almost immediately on October 6, 1928.

Unfortunately Glenn and Helen could not have children, so they adopted a boy and a girl, Steve Miller and Jonnie Miller. From my understanding, both still reap some financial rewards from Glenn's early works and recordings.

Glenn's in-laws were enamoured of him and the respect was always mutual. Woody Herman once told me that they mortgaged their home to help finance Glenn's second attempt at forming a band.

One of the truths in the movie The Glenn Miller Story was the love and affection Jimmy Stewart and June Allyson displayed to one another. And, yes, Helen Miller was there to back the story up as she visited the movie set every day during filming.

Glenn and Helen moved into an apartment in Astoria, Queens, New York, a suburb then of New York City. They later moved to New Jersey on the advice of their financial manager David Mackay.

A New Kind of Music in the Rainbow Room

"A band ought to have a sound all of its own. It ought to have a personality." —Glenn Miller

Glenn Miller's foundation of careful planning, precision playing, all around discipline, and the ability to express serious musical emotion, drew him deeply into the craft. It allowed him to organize and manage the new Dorsey Brothers musical organization in 1934, remaining for one year, leaving them just before the Dorsey's infamous break-up, to work with the new Ray Noble Orchestra, put-

Ray Noble and his Orchestra in the Rainbow Room
(R. Grudens collection)

ting together Noble's first American band that performed up on the 65th floor of Rockefeller Center's famed Rainbow Room. His supervision of Britain's prestigious Ray Noble Orchestra, and the New Mayfair Orchestra's first U.S. tour, and a Columbia Records commission for arranging, were important to Glenn's development in forming his own first band.

Admittedly, however, Glenn was not the perfect trombone player:

"If I could play as well as Tommy Dorsey, I'd star myself and others in the band, otherwise I'll have to make the band great by arrangements and precision playing."

Bobby Hackett, Glenn's stellar trumpet player: "I think he would have traded everything to play as good as Jack Teagarden or Tommy (Dorsey), but he never became jealous and even happily wrote material for each of them."

It was about this time that Glenn was studying under Professor Joseph Schillinger, a noted music teacher and theorist who had tutored both George Gershwin and Vernon Duke. While studying, Glenn had written an arrangement as part of an exercise lesson for trombone that he would translate into his future theme. This composition was later named "Moonlight Serenade."

Earlier, through an inadvertent musical director's choice at a rehearsal, and to the unexpected absence of one of his trumpet players while rehearsing Ray Noble's band at the Rainbow Room, Glenn directed stellar clarinetist Johnny Mince to play the trumpet part of a chart with the clarinet. That moment punctuated Glenn's long sought after special "sound." Everyone in the band knew it when Glenn's face lit up like a Christmas tree.

Glenn's First Band

By 1937, Glenn had decided he would form his own band, but after a slow start it painfully fell to financial difficulties that forced him to abandon the effort. Somehow, the Glenn Miller Orchestra failed to attract public interest at that moment of "time and chance" enough to succeed. The band's low point occurred at a one-nighter when Glenn received only $125.00 for the use of his entire band at Bowdoin College, in Brunswick, Maine. The failed attempt to continue his first band drove Glenn almost to desperation. He returned to his home in Jackson Heights, New York, from York Pennsylvania, where the band played its last gig before disbanding. Uncertain of his next step, Glenn thought he would never have the chance again to form his long sought-after dream band. Glenn advised his hardworking musicians to take a rest and promised to call them when he re-formed. The better players quickly found new positions. But, undaunted and encouraged by some fellow musicians, Glenn valiantly tried again the following year, and with financial help from his in-laws, who were willing to re-mortgage their home to help their much admired son-in-law, and their loving daughter, Helen, Glenn reformed his band.

Glenn's Successful Band
Riding the Heights

One of Glenn's favorite musicians, saxist Hal McIntyre, recounts the story of the emergence of Glenn's second band:

"After the first band broke up, I took all the equipment up to our farm in Cromwell, Connecticut, and got a job in a factory and played with my own band at night. I used to call up Glenn every Sunday afternoon at one and try to argue him into starting the band once again. But he'd always say,

'nothing doing,' and that he had gone through $18,000.00 too fast to want to go back into the band business.

"Well, one afternoon Glenn was driving through Cromwell and he called me from a diner. I went over to see him, and we talked about starting up the band again. At first he said, no. But I detected some resistance and kept on working at him until he gave in.

Hal McIntyre

'O.K.' he said, 'we start rehearsals at the New Haven studio next week.' Boy was I happy!"

"Glenn's good friend Tommy Dorsey told him to break up that old, unproductive band and start out fresh with a bunch of young kids who would have more enthusiasm and wouldn't mind rehearsing and working hard on something, and that's what he did." —Tex Beneke

This time the new band succeeded beyond Glenn's wildest dreams. To maintain absolute control he became tougher on his musicians and in his business practices. He had learned lessons the hard way. No longer would he tolerate misbehaving, drinking, lateness, indifference, or pandering to "prima donnas" among the musicians.

From the 'old band' Glenn retained pianist and friend Chummy MacGregor, his favorite bass player Rolly Bundock, trumpeter Bob Price, sax player and friend Hal McIntyre, and a very young and eager vocalist, Ray Eberle, brother of Bob Eberly of the Jimmy Dorsey band, whom he freshly hired for his first employment singing with any band.

When the newly organized Glenn Miller Orchestra opened at the Glen Island Casino in New Rochelle, New

York on May 17, 1939, after a successful engagement at the Meadowbrook in New Jersey, it broadcast over both the NBC and Mutual networks, measurably increasing the band's national exposure. The 1800 fans that crowded the opening broke all existing attendance records, inflating the band's prominence.

Glenn Miller went on to lead the most popular and best-remembered dance band of the Big Band Swing era. Glenn was an exceptionally intense, ambitious perfectionist. His success was built upon the band's precise execution of meticulously crafted arrangements of carefully chosen musical material, rather than in the propulsive swing or jazz solo improvisation school of playing, which he was content to leave to other bands.

Glenn Joins the Army Air Force

Why did Glenn Miller disband the most popular and the most profitable band in music history to join the Army Air Force when he didn't have to, as he was over the draft age limit? It meant relinquishing millions of dollars of revenue in motion picture and recording contract opportunities. The truth is Glenn wanted to stand up and be counted when his country was at war. He had all the selfish reasons not to go. But he went, because he needed to serve his country in any way possible to satisfy his desire to be patriotic. Performing music with a great orchestra was the natural way for Glenn to serve. He wanted to slip in his two-cents worth, or else. Before entering active duty, there would be a few more personal appearances and broadcasts remaining to be completed.

Glenn had also been aware that many of his players would be drafted, too, and that a damaging recording ban was expected to take effect on August 1, 1942. The American Federation of Musicians, a union headed by its President, James Petrillo, was openly crusading against bands making records and releasing transcriptions of shows for broadcast.

He argued that recorded music was infringing on attendance records of live music, and accordingly, was determined to place a choke-hold on the record business.

Glenn, like other bandleaders and vocalists, rushed into the recording studios for some hastily scheduled sessions that, for him, included "That Old Black Magic," and "Jukebox Saturday Night," with the Modernaires, which almost wasn't released. Apparently, some operators of jukeboxes felt insulted by the lyrics. Jukebox operators purchased over 50 percent of all records produced.

Glenn Miller moved on to even greater heights upon forming the Army Air Force Band. The music world was caught off-guard by his decision to quit his civilian band in favor of forming an Army Air Force band. He had to break numerous engagements and disengage contracts, but his visions of directing a magnificent and instrumentally sophisticated giant sized orchestra was not to be denied him.

Captain Glenn Miller with the Army Air Force Band
in the Yale Bowl, New Haven, Conn. - 1943

Glenn in Atlantic City
1938

Glenn MIller and his Orchestra - Photographed on Hamid's Million Dollar Steel Pier in Atlantic City, NJ - August 1938

On the Boardwalk

GLENN MILLER ORCHESTRA 1938

August 1938 at Hamid's Million Dollar Pier in Atlantic City

Trombones - Brad Jenney, Al Mastren, Glenn Miller
Trumpets - Johnny Austin, Bob Price, Louis Mucci
Clarinet - Willie Schwartz
Pianist - Chummy MacGregor
Saxists - Tex Beneke, Stan Aronson,
Hal McIntyre, Bill Stegmeyer
Drums - Bob Spangler
Bass - Rolly Bundock
Vocalists - Linda Keene, Ray Eberle

GLENN MILLER ORCHESTRA 1942

Saxophone - Mose Klink, Tex Beneke, Skip Martin,
Willie Schwartz, Ernie Caceres
Trumpets - John Best, Mickey McMickle,
Steve Lipkins, Billy May
Trombones - Jimmy Priddy, Frank D'Anolfo,
Paul Tanner, Glenn Miller
Rhythms - Guitar - Bobby Hackett
Piano - Chummy MacGregor
Drums - Moe Purtill
Bass - Doc Goldberg

Martin Block

Martin Block Host of WNEW's Make Believe Ballroom
(Courtesy WNEW)

The Magic of Martin Block and WNEW

"Where The Melody Lingers On"

Radio station WNEW, New York, became the musicians friend since the day President Franklin D. Roosevelt pressed a button in his White House study illuminating a golden lamp in the WNEW, New York, transmitter room at exactly 9:00 PM on February 13, 1934.

Immediately following, soprano Yvonne D'Arle sang the "Star-Spangled Banner" and the Governor of New Jersey, A. Harry Moore, delivered an address of welcome. From that moment on, music claimed the emerging, great radio station, WNEW. A young lady vocalist, Theresa Stabile, who went on to fame as Dolly Dawn with the Dawn Patrol, broadcast from a Newark, New Jersey studio, performing with a live orchestra, and Kay Reed, once organist for the famed Roxy Theater in New York, joined the station and remained the house organist for many years.

Ms. Bernice Judis, General Manager of the station, operated with great vision and is credited for introducing the first all-night radio show, originating news around the clock, and giving the legendary Martin Block the opportunity to become the nation's first disc jockey. They say she loved radios like some men loved cars. And, it was the prolific Martin Block who first began broadcasting his recorded music, which, at the time, was created to allow studio musicians time to rehearse between live performances. Block was the first announcer to personalize records, inspiring famed New York Daily Mirror columnist Walter Winchell to coin the phrase "disc jockey." And, Martin Block originated the Make Believe Ballroom in New York on February 3, 1935. He borrowed the idea from radio personality Al Jarvis during a visit to Los Angeles where Jarvis hosted a similar show. And it was TV icon Joe Franklin who first began his own legendary career serving as Martin Block's record picker.

"Martin Block," Joe Franklin told me during a recent conversation at Hofstra University on Long Island during the November, 2002, Bing Crosby Cultural Conference, "would introduce a record with his great wit, his inspiring voice, and that record would grow some magical luster, captivate listeners and make them buy the record or two. He had an ear for New York's musical wants and needs. He had an amazing ability to know what was going to succeed and what would satisfy the public."

His program seemed to create winners. Block would emcee live broadcasts of the big bands at places like Glen Island Casino in New Rochelle, New York, the premier venue for a the big bands of the day, like Glenn Miller's fine orchestra. The first theme music for the show was "Sugar Blues" by Clyde McCoy, who had a band in the Midwest. Glenn Miller, winner of the Make Believe Ballroom 1940 popularity poll, recorded "It's Make Believe Ballroom Time," which became the show's permanent theme following Glenn Miller's disappearance. In December, 1944. Martin Block and Glenn Miller had become pretty close friends.

L-R, Glenn, Martin Block, Tex Beneke and the Modernaires
(*R. Grudens collection*)

IT'S MAKE BELIEVE BALLROOM TIME

Harold Green, Mickey Stoner and Martin Block

It's Make Believe Ballroom Time.
Put all your cares away
All the bands are here
To bring good cheer your way
It's Make Believe Ballroom Time
And free to everyone,
It's no time to fret
Your dial is set for fun
Just close your eyes and visualize
In your solitude
Your favorite bands
Are on the stands
And Mr. Miller puts you
"In the Mood"
It's Make Believe Ballroom Time
The hour of sweet romance
Here's your Make Believe Ballroom
Come on, children,
Let's dance
Let's dance.

The format of the program was to welcome bands and singers into an imaginary ballroom with a "revolving stage." Performers remained under a crystal chandelier for 15 minutes while they performed and millions of people visualized the ballroom in their imagination. Martin made each listener feel like an intimate confidant, sharing his special musical world. When William B. Williams and I worked a live version of the Make Believe Ballroom at Westbury, New York's, Westbury Music Fair in the mid-eighties, he explained it further:

"Martin Block's ability to predict winners from new releases was absolutely uncanny and gained him considerable influence among the top performers of the day. His show became the first showcase for disc jockeys and the major promotion channel for the phonograph industry. That's why here, in 1984, we still carry on with the Make Believe Ballroom and are here to showcase it in front of the listening public. Glenn Miller's music mixed with Tony Bennett and all the other great stars is still an influence after all these years and that's why they are here tonight."

William B., as he was affectionately known, was the current keeper of the Make Believe Ballroom flame, and had been it's star since he took over from host Jerry Marshall in 1957. William B. began his show each morning with the salutation "Hello, World!"

Martin Block's broadcast studio at WNEW, where he helped make Glenn Miller's band the number one band in the nation, actually was furnished complete with a chandelier, red velvet chair with black linoleum on the floor.

"It's your Make Believe Ballroom, You and You and especially You," Block would say during his 3 1/2 hour daily broadcast. Martin Block's vast record collection was donated to New York University after his death on September 19, 1967.

After my friend, William B. Williams, passed on in 1986 after a bout with cancer, I received a note from song star Margaret Whiting:

"....remembering our meeting at Westbury a few years ago with William B. God, I miss him—as a friend—but, most of all, I miss him on the air. WNEW just isn't the same any more. I know they're trying, but the whole kind of programming they used to do with Kenton, Miller, Harry James, and Crosby, and every big band is just gone."

It got worse. WNEW went off the air December 2, 1992. The great radio voices of Jim Lowe, Jerry Marshall, Bob Jones and Jonathan Schwartz with echoes of the Glenn Miller Orchestra and the other great bands was stilled. For a while in 1995, radio station WQEW went on the air to try and recover, but not for long. Soon, it too was gone forever.

Over on Long Island, Jack Ellsworth, whose daily WALK radio 10-12 morning show, "Memories in Melody," remains on the air, may be one of the last such programs who features Glenn Miller radio broadcast air-checks and early recordings of all the great bands and vocalists daily.

VARIETY POLL OF TWENTY STATIONS NATIONWIDE SUMMER 1939 ADDED TO THE POLL OF NY WNEW, MARTIN BLOCK'S MAKE BELIEVE BALLROOM. VOTED BY LISTENERS, REFLECTING THE BIG BAND FAVORITES

GLENN MILLER 44,446

TOMMY DORSEY 23,645

BENNY GOODMAN 16,321

SAMMY KAYE 13,854

KAY KYSER 11,619

GENE KRUPA 10,104

CHARLIE BARNET 8,469

JIMMY DORSEY 7,537

ARTIE SHAW 5,532

JAN SAVITT 4,377

PLUNKETT'S
The Trombone Club

Artie Shaw once told me about Plunkett's: *"We hung out there. It was a hole-in-the-wall joint under the Sixth Avenue EL on West 53rd Street at Ninth Avenue, where I met a music conductor from CBS who got me an audition and a part-time job with Red Nichol's Band. As a result, I got to play first saxophone in the CBS staff orchestra. I was only twenty."*

Plunkett's, a speakeasy on West Fifty-third Street, was the way station, the hangout, the boardroom, the shape-up outlet for the great New York musicians: Jack Teagarden, Artie Shaw, Tommy Dorsey, Benny Goodman, Jimmy Dorsey, Glenn Miller, among others. The password to get in was always "Tommy Dorsey sent me."

When music contractors wanted musicians for this or that gig, or for a radio show, legitimate theater, or recording studio, he could find one hanging out at Plunkett's. Especially trombone players. Plunkett's had a call board always covered with messages. The phone consistently rang and drinks were generally paid for by a musician who had a few bucks to spare that particular day. The next day someone else plunked down some momentarily unclaimed dollars.

Late in any particular afternoon, you'd see Bix Biedercecke and Frank Teschmaker napping in a booth, perhaps after a tough recording session, or a return trip from an out-of-town gig, but, it was said they awoke as soon as Tommy and Jimmy Dorsey's fights started. There were a number of passwords used at Plunkett's in those days, according to Esquire's 1947 Jazzbook. There were two booths in the small back room, but they were seldom utilized except for a siesta or for the disquieting, occasional visit of an angry wife. Each day the barreled beer arrived in a different truck; a florist's delivery car, a milk wagon, or even a hearse. Eddie Condon's dressing room, an icebox Tommy Dorsey always talked about, was loaded to the ceiling with thousands of dollars worth of instruments—everybody's—from Tommy Dorsey's famous collection of gold saxophones to Pee Wee Russell's crud-caked clarinet, or Bix Beiderbecke's old cornet stored and forgotten about in a corduroy sack, and even a fiddle of Joe Venuti and Jack Teagarden's and Glenn Miller's old trombones.

The camaraderie at Plunkett's was something special—maybe surreal. Why, when the Dorsey Brothers started their orchestra, Jimmy Plunkett was their manager. The bar was about ten feet long and on the shelves above were a half-dozen nondescript beer steins. In the telephone book Plunkett's was listed as The Trombone Club.

Artie Shaw: *"We hung out at Plunkett's when there was nothing to do, nothing to play, or while we were waiting for something to happen. It usually improved our attitude and provided some needed laughs."*

THE RCA BLUEBIRD
BANDLEADERS QUESTIONAIRE

Glenn Miller filled out a questionnaire when he applied for an RCA Victor/Bluebird contract to record in 1938. His manager at the time was Cy Shribman. These are the exact questions and exact answers personally provided by Glenn himself. They are typed here because the original questionnaire is very faded and difficult to read.

Name: **Glenn Miller**
Type of professional work: **Orchestra Leader**
Full Name in private life: **Alton Glenn Miller**
Address: 3780 88th Street, Jackson Heights, L.I.
Phone Number: **Havemeyer 6 - 0671**
Your instrument, if any, or if vocal, what voice:
    Trombone and arranger
How long have you been a Victor or Bluebird
    recording artist: **One month**
Name of your personal manager, if any: **Cy**
    Shribman
His address: **799 7th Ave, NYC**
Month, Day and year of birth: **March 1st, 1904**
City and state of birth: **Clarinda, Iowa**
Father's name: **Lewis Elmer Miller**
Mother's maiden name: **Matty Lou Cavender**
Father's Occupation: **Building contractor**
Was either parent talented: **No**
What was your childhood ambition:
    Professional Baseball Player
Who was your childhood hero in fiction:
    Horatio Alger
In real life: **Teddy Roosevelt**
Did your parents object to your vocational ambi-
    tions: **My trombone playing often drove**
    my father to quieter haunts away from
    home.

What was the first stage play you remember seeing: **The "Last Mile" with Spencer Tracy**

What was the first concert or recital: **Hansel and Gretel, Chicago Opera**

Describe an early experience in entertaining audiences: **In high school and college I would gladly play trombone anytime and anywhere and appeared in the usual high school plays.**

Were any present day prominent artists among your early friends: **Benny Goodman, Tommy and Jimmy Dorsey were early music associates.**

What was a chief influence in early life: **Phonograph**

Were you encouraged or discouraged in your talent development by family or friends: **Encouraged by my mother, discouraged by college associates.**

Did you excel in any sport: **High School football**

Other extracurricular activities: **Band and Orchestra**

College Fraternity: **Sigma Nu**

How long have you studied music: **Studied arranging two years**

With whom: **Dr. Joseph Schillinger, NYC**

Are you still studying: **No**

Where and when did you make your professional debut: **With Boyd Sentor's Orch in Denver, CO.**

At what age. **17**

Any special incidents that occurred: **I remember following a man with a trombone under his arm, until he went into a night club and thinking my ambitions would** be realized if I were good enough to work in that club.

Are you performing for radio now: **My band is broadcast weekly on Columbia Mutual and National chains 7-12 times weekly.**

What one person has particularly aided you in your work: **Tommy Dorsey.**

What was the first job of any kind you held: **Milking a cow—salary 1.00 per week.**

Tell us about your recording career: **Have been making recordings in New York for the past eight years.**

Outside of your musical career, what other work have you done: **Soda jerk while going to high school. Worked in a sugar factory while going to high school.**

Did you ever have "mike fright:" **Yes**

Do you still have it: **Yes, at times.**

If so, please describe: **Drying of the mouth. Shaking of the knees. Blankness of the mind.**

How have you overcome it: **I have practically overcome it by developing confidence in myself and my band. Deep abdominal breathing is helpful.**

What do you consider the turning point of your career: **Forming my own band.**

Have you appeared in the movies, vaudeville, plays or musical shows: **No.**

Are you married: **Yes!**

To Whom: **Mrs. Miller**

When: **(left blank)**

List your musical compositions: **My theme "Moonlight Serenade." "Doin' the Jive," "Sold American," "Sometime."**

What form of travel do you enjoy: **Train**

Do you own a car: **Yes**

Ever flown a plane: **No**
If not, ever wished to: **Yes**
Where would you prefer to live: **New York—most everything desirable is in New York.**
Where would you spend summers: **Colorado.**
Do you believe in breaks of fortune: **Yes**
Describe a break that shaped your career: **The interest Ben Pollack showed in me when he hired me to play and arrange for his band.**
Are you even-tempered: **Yes, fairly**
Do you like to write letters: **No, can't think of anything to write.**
How do you spend your days off: **Arranging**
Have you ever had a serious illness or injury: **No**
Any narrow escapes from death: **No**
What recording artist do you admire: **Tommy Dorsey**
What is you favorite popular song: **"You Go to my head."**
What is your favorite quotation: **"It don't mean a thing if it ain't got that swing."**
If you had a million dollars, what would you do with it: **I'd have the best band in the world.**

Well, Glenn eventually did, and, without a million dollars.

"HE LIKES JITTERBUGS"

Glenn Miller scorned the quick "road to success" . . .
for him, slow-but-steady won the race

"WE'VE just signed Glenn Miller and his orchestra," the proprietors of the Glen Island Casino told us, "and we're worried a little. After all, he's just beginning and—well—this has been such a hectic year for bands. So many flash-in-the-pan outfits. . . ."

Even the fact that Glenn Miller's outfit had just before broken attendance records at Frank Dailey's Meadowbrook Club wasn't comforting. Or that Miller's Bluebird recordings ranked among the best sellers.

A few weeks later we visited the Glen Island Casino again. The proprietors looked happy, but worn. "Gosh, we can hardly handle the crowds," was their plaint. "We don't know where to put them. We've never had anything quite like this before. Even last year with Larry Clinton and before that with the Casa Loma band and the Dorseys." Glenn Miller had shattered records again —brought the biggest crowds that had ever stormed the popular Westchester dining and dancing rendezvous.

That, in a nutshell, is a picture of the wild acclaim with which Glenn Miller's music has been received.

A most romantic way to tell the story of Glenn Miller would be to write in glowing terms of a Young Lochinvar who came out of the West in a blaze of glory to dazzle the world with the brilliance of his immediate accomplishments. Since Glenn comes from Clarinda, Iowa, and is today one of the brightest stars in the orchestral firmament, we could take advantage of what is known as "poetic license" to skip lightly over the time that elapsed between his arrival in New York and his recent rise to fame.

That would do for the sake of glamour. But it would do a great injustice to Glenn and the years he spent in preparation for the success he enjoys today. For Glenn's is a story of patience, determination, courage and travail.

So far as is generally known, Glenn Miller is an overnight success. To the public he is a sensation who skyrocketed from the depths of nonentity to the brilliance of a position in which he challenges Benny Goodman, Artie Shaw and Tommy Dorsey for the supremacy of the swing world. To those of us who didn't know Glenn before, this all happened faster than you could say Bix Beiderbecke.

Actually, however, this is not true. Glenn has been dreaming of and leading up to this for more than ten years while he wrote arrangements and played his trombone in other bands.

"I've always wanted to have my own band," he said. "But the kind of a band that would mean something, not just a group of musicians. I could have started ten years ago. So what? My band would probably never have meant a thing and chances are I'd still be playing all the honky-tonks this side of Passaic."

Miller, however, is long-sighted, cautious, particular. He made up his mind that he would never seek a quick cash-in and

run the risk of dubious fame. He had watched too many others fade into oblivion, their careers shattered.

Unknown to most of us, perhaps, Glenn was nevertheless known and respected among his colleagues as a "musicians' musician." He was in constant demand for his prowess with the trombone and his unusual talent as an arranger. Bandleaders confided in him. He was a good listener and they respected his opinions. For many years he has enjoyed a reputation for his uncanny ability to find the right man to fill gaps in bands.

"Glenn, I need a good tenor man," a batoneer would confide. "If I could find just the right man it would improve my outfit immensely."

"I'll see what I can do for you," he would say quietly. The next day a new tenor sax man would report to the troubled leader. Invariably he would prove to be just what was needed to bolster the lagging band. Miller performed this service for the Dorseys, Goodman, Glen Gray and others who are today famous. In this way he had a hand in the organizing of many of the current important orchestras and his distinctive arrangements helped establish their styles.

When Ray Noble came to these shores, sans his own orchestra, which was forced to remain in England because of our labor laws, he went into a huddle with Glenn Miller, whose reputation as a band maker had been relayed to him. Glenn became his chief arranger and assistant bandleader, assuming the responsibility of organizing the band. He stayed with Noble several years, then he went back to radio orchestras as a trombonist.

All the time that he sat, long-legged and bespectacled, playing his trombone on various bandstands, Glenn thought of and stored away original ideas for musical tricks. He kept them secret, as he did the revolutionary arrangements that were years ahead of the times, until he would have an opportunity to use them for his own band. A year ago he decided he was ready to start out on his own.

Batoneers, grateful for the assistance he had lent them, recommended men and offered other kinds of help. Glenn had worked hard turning out a repertoire of arrangements and the style of his band was soon set. He played break-in dates at the Paradise Restaurant, Atlantic City and Asbury Park. Band bookers still showed but minor interest, but Miller knew he had something good. He continued to polish, insisting on the highest degree of perfection attainable. When he returned to the Paradise for a second time he had added blonde Marion Hutton and Ray Eberle as vocalists. There were other additions and corrections. He was determined to make a good showing that time. And the inevitable happened.

People are talking about the musical tricks that identify the Miller band on the air and on recordings. The "saxatones," for instance, in which the clarinet and fourth (Continued on page 25)

"He Likes Jitterbugs"

(Continued from page 10)

alto play melody an octave apart, with the other alto and two tenor saxes filling in the harmony. "It sounds like an organ," wrote one Miller fan. And the "brass choir" which Miller devised for what he calls "pretty tunes."

Asked about these things, Miller says, "I thought of them long ago. I've even used variations of them before. And I've been planning to feature them some day in my own band."

Glenn likes to talk about the days when he joined Ben Pollack's band, fresh out of Colorado University. He played alongside of Benny Goodman and Gene Krupa in that outfit. Even way back then he played swing. Bix Beiderbecke heard he was one of the finest trombone "ride men" and, when he heard for himself, was so sold on the youth that he used him in the famous Beiderbecke recording combo.

Miller's other claim to distinction among baton wavers is that, unlike the rest of them, he *likes* to play for jitterbugs, likes their appreciation of swing, but refuses to play for them all night. If he looks like a college professor to you, blame it on his glasses and his mild, soft-spoken manner.

The Miller Gang's All Here

Glenn Miller and his Orchestra - Back row - L-R: on Trumpet: Johnny Best, Billy May. On Drum: Maurice Purtill. On Bass: Trigger Alpert. On Guitar: Jack Lathrop.

Second Row - On Trumpet: Ray Anthony, Wade McMickle. On the far right on Saxophone: Tex Beneke, Al Klink.

Front Row - On Trombone: Paul Tanner, Jimmy Priddy, Frank D'Annolfo. Vocal: Ralph Brewster, Hal Dickinson, Ray Eberle, Chuck Goldstein, Billy Conway. On Piano: Chummy McGregor. On Saxophone: Ernie Caceres, Hal McIntyre, Willie Schwartz. Front and Center - Glenn Miller.

(R. Grudens collection)

Johnny Mince

J. Muenzenberger and the Truth about the Glenn Miller Sound

Glenn: *"When I was with Ray Noble in New York, one day my trumpet player, Pee Wee Erwin had to leave suddenly and the trumpet player who replaced him couldn't play the high stuff. In desperation, I assigned those B-flat trumpet parts to Johnny Mince on B-flat clarinet and doubled the clarinet lead with Danny D'Andrea, a violinist who doubled on reeds, an octave lower on sax. That's how the clarinet-lead sound started."*

When the Glenn Miller Orchestra opened at the Glen Island Casino in New Rochelle, New York on May 17, 1939, it broadcast on both the NBC and Mutual networks giving them exposure that vastly increased the band's already rising success. Eighteen hundred fans crowded into that most important dance hall to punctuate the bands rise to the big time. The jitterbugs, the kids who hung around the bandstand. The engagement lasted until August 18th.

Glenn Miller had finally hit it really big. Success as a bandleader had evaded him for years

Johnny Mince
(R. Grudens collection)

until he found his "sound" and grew confident with it , even augmenting his brass and trombone sections, adding two more full-sounding sections.

Clarinet player Johnny Mince tells the story of just how that sound was discovered. In the days before Frank Sinatra began crooning soft tunes for Tommy Dorsey, and Glenn Miller sat in the third row playing trombone for bandleader Ray Noble, there emerged an immensely talented clarinet player named John Henry Muenzenberger, who hailed from Chicago and settled on Long Island. You knew him as Johnny Mince.

Johnny began his career at age seventeen in New York with the Joe Haymes band that later became the Buddy Rogers band. Johnny's friend, Glenn Miller, who was managing the band for the Englishman, Ray Noble, signed him and Pee Wee Erwin into the organization after Buddy quit to join J. Arthur Rank in Hollywood and Noble took over. Glenn was also the band's arranger in those days. Players like Ziggy Elman, Buddy DeFranco, Davey Tough, Bunny Berigan, and Buddy Rich, along with arrangers Paul Weston, Axel Stordahl, and Sy Oliver were in the band. It was the beginning of the Big Band Era for one of the best and most talented grass roots organizations.

Inadvertently, Johnny became the catalyst for the original Glenn Miller sound. One Tuesday afternoon in 1981, at the Three Village Inn in Stonybrook, New York, Johnny Mince and I sat down and he told me the true story, and it clearly differed from the silly Hollywood version portrayed in the *Glenn Miller Story* where it showed a trumpet player bumping his lip and then a clarinet player taking his spot in the band and thereby creating a reversal of instruments.

"The truth is that we were rehearsing with Ray Noble's band at the Rainbow Room on the 65th floor in Radio City. Trumpet player Pee Wee Erwin called in sick, so Glenn asked me to play the trumpet part with the clarinet. 'I want to see what it sounds like,' he said. "He had been trying this 'sound' idea for years, but he didn't think to use the clarinet on top—playing a double with the tenor below. Pee Wee's playing had a wonderful high register that would play those very high notes with the saxophone voice underneath him. As it turned out, I don't think we went through the first eight bars and everyone knew that was the sound that Glenn Miller had been searching for all those years. It was written all over his face. That was the beginning of the famous Glenn Miller sound that punctuated his success as the most popular band of the era."

Another tale, told by Johnny Mince, about his friend Glenn Miller.

"One night up in that same Rainbow Room with Noble, before we got on the stand, several of us were warming up—Glenn comes up and says he had written a tune (a lesson composed for his arranging teacher) and asked us to go over it. It was a beautiful thing and Glenn later asked us to come down to Broadway the next day to record it. So we met in one of those studios on 49th Street, and for just twenty-five cents recorded Glenn's immortal tune, "Moonlight Serenade." Little did we know...and I wonder what value that little plastic disc would hold today."

Jukebox Saturday Night

Glenn at the Jukebox - 1941
(R. Grudens collection)

UNDERSTANDING the GLENN MILLER SOUND

DOUBLING A MELODY ON SAXOPHONE WITH A CLARINET AN OCTAVE HIGHER, WITH SEAMLESS ARRANGEMENTS AND PLAYING SWINGING RIFF TUNES LIKE "IN THE MOOD," AND "TUXEDO JUNCTION."

THIS METHOD WITH EXPLANATIONS CAN BE FOLLOWED MORE CAREFULLY IN HIS 1943 BOOK, "GLENN MILLER'S METHODS OF ORCHESTRAL ARRANGING."

"Note, for example, his unique style of scoring for one clarinet and four saxes, and then some of the moving background figures he writes for the brass to play into hats, and you'll get a pretty good idea of the swell, set style upon which he and his men are working."

GLENN'S METHODS
FOR ARRANGING

In 1943 Glenn wrote a book describing his method for orchestral arranging.

GLENN, from his book: *"As a young arranger, I was always searching for some work that actually described the process involved in making orchestral arrangements. Many comprehensive volumes have been written about harmony, theory, counterpoint, orchestration and composition, but to my knowledge, no book has ever been written which actually told how to make an arrangement. That is why I have written this book. If it in any way solves this problem for ambitious young arrangers, it shall have fulfilled the purpose for which it is intended."*

This unique book is filled with actual arranging charts covering many of the important compositions that make up the original Glenn Miller book, which now surpasses 1700 pcs, as witnessed when I recently visited the members of the orchestra and their leader, Larry O'Brien. Because of continual use, many of the sheets are dog-eared and worn, but still provide each musician with an exact score to follow. As we know, Glenn had always demanded his musicians follow those charts precisely as they were written, a tradition current leader Larry O'Brien has continued.

We present here a few instrument charts that provide signature and sound in concert key, signature and same scale as written for the instrument, playing range as written for the instrument, playing range and actual sound written in concert, as well as sample excerpts of some of those scores.

These terms may mean little to anyone who does not play an instrument, but illustrate for the non-musician how Glenn arranged some of the uses of the various sections as employed in his dance orchestra.

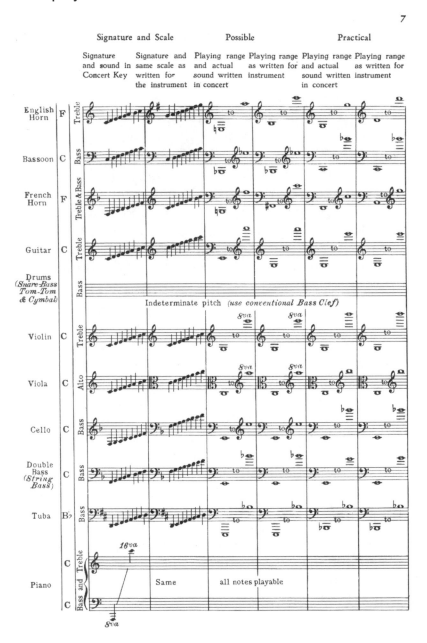

INSTRUMENT CHART

	Signature and Scale		Possible		Practical	
Instrument / KEY / CLEF	Signature and sound in Concert Key	Signature and same scale as written for the instrument	Playing range and actual sound written in concert	Playing range as written for instrument	Playing range and actual sound written in concert	Playing range as written for instrument

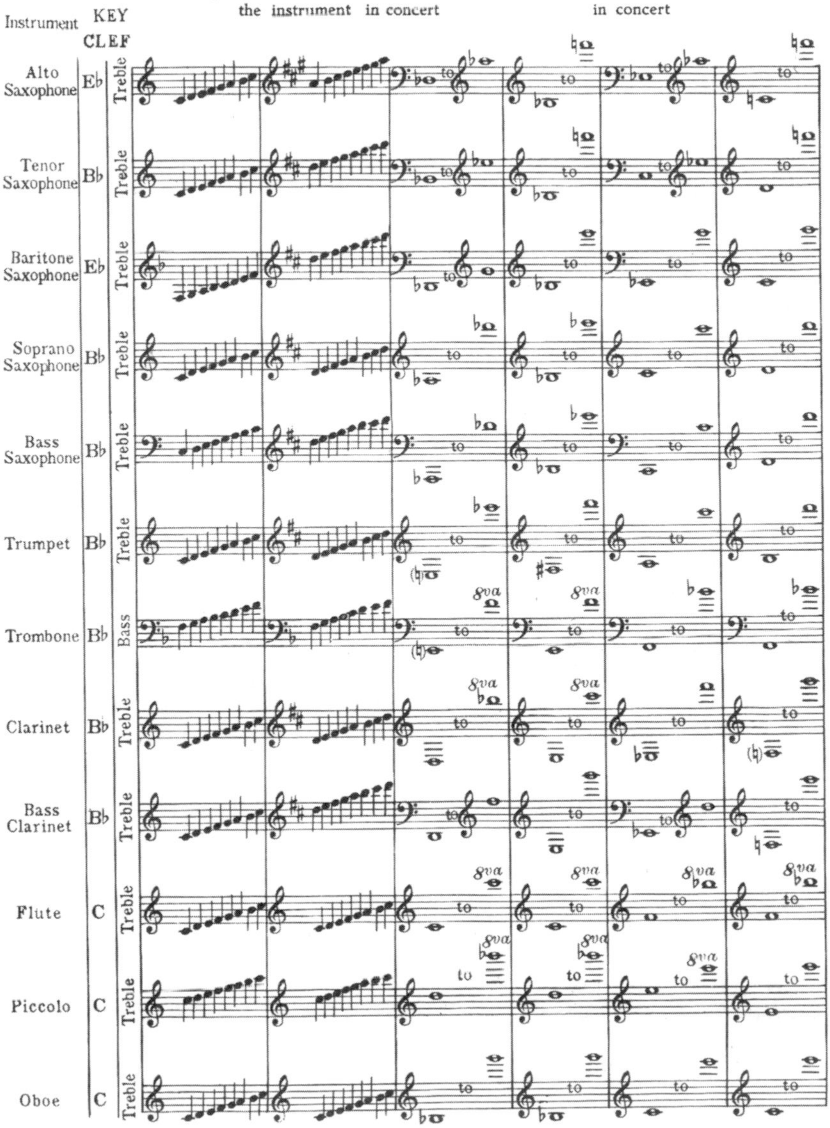

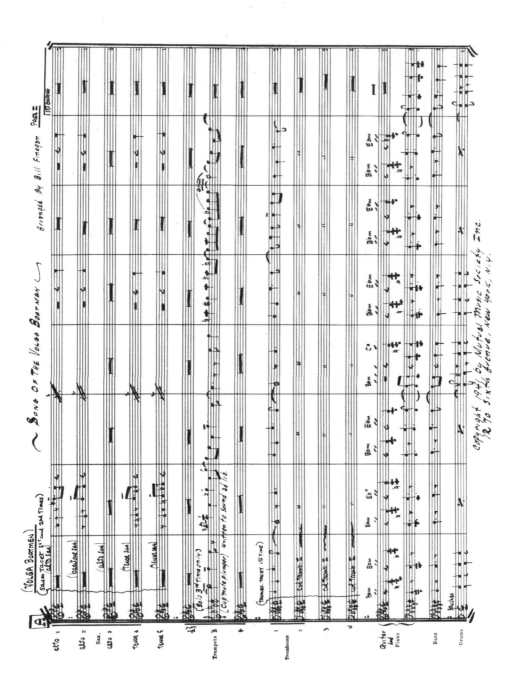

The American Band of the Allied Expeditionery Force in England led by Major Glenn Miller.

THE AMERICAN BAND OF THE ALLIED EXPEDITIONERY FORCE

"Though it may sound shocking at first, it turns out that Miller's fabulously famous 1939-1942 band actually represented a stylistic detour, which ironically World War II allowed him to correct with his Air Force Orchestra." —Gunther Schuller, *The Swing Era*.

Performances of Glenn Miller's 42 piece *American Band of the Allied Expeditionery Force* were always enthusiastically greeted by American G.I.'s. Once kids, now turned men, caught up in an ongoing and immense World War that was, at last, turning around favorably for the Allies, they listened to Glenn's music that had been shifted from live performances and malt shop jukeboxes in America to venues in English towns and villages that lay across a vast ocean where they began playing concerts anywhere American G.I.'s were stationed and poised for war. This phenomenon has, for millions of Americans, created an undiminished aura of nostalgic music unprecedented in music history that remains to this day.

The band was really a concert orchestra composed of the usual Miller dance band group of nineteen odd musicians, plus a French horn and a twenty piece string ensemble. A magnificent group with the best musicians available. Not considered a 'jazz' unit, the band was really a massive entertainment band that played a great variety of musical numbers.

During one of those open air concerts, General Jimmy Doolittle, Commanding General of the U.S. 8th Army Air Force, climbed aboard a temporary constructed outdoor stage and personally honored Glenn Miller:

> *"Captain Miller, next to a letter from home, your organization is the greatest morale-builder in the European Theater of Operations. "*

...to thunderous applause!

Formerly the Army Air Force Band, Glenn's great musical entertainment enterprise spent three hard-working months performing in concerts and continuous broadcasts, employing almost every available musician he could find. The American Band of the Allied Expeditionery Force operated in London, England, and was sponsored and funded by America's Office of War Information to provide entertainment and to disseminate propaganda that was broadcast directly to Germany, along with a vocal effort, to convince young German soldiers to give up the fight. This was a propaganda program undertaken before the buildup for, what we now know was, the "D" Day invasion.

The band's first broadcast at the end of April, 1944, with cooperation from British Broadcasters sponsoring American entertainers, included vocalists Bing Crosby and Dinah Shore. Both stars would read phonetic German to introduce their songs. As an aside, the song "Is You Is or Is You Ain't My Baby" translated, became "Bist du oder bist nicht mein Baby."

Glenn's orchestra recorded at the famous Abbey Road Studio, then known as the HMV studio. Almost all Glenn's hits would be broadcast during these sessions.

Sure, the great new band was strictly G.I., but was undoubtedly and essentially a Glenn Miller musical event, as many of his civilian band musicians were on hand to perform; including pianist Mel Powell, drummer Ray McKinley, clarinetist Peanuts Hucko, bassist Trigger Alpert, saxist Hank Freeman, trumpeters Bernie Privin and Zeke Zarchy. Johnny Desmond performed the vocals. Artie Malvin and the Crew Chiefs shared the Modernaires style vocal chores.

Glenn's G.I.'s

Somewhere in England

Eyewitness

Tom Tatarian

Tom Tatarian, eyewitness: During an early 1944 concert held in an airplane hangar in the town of Royston, eighty-one year old former B-17 tailgunner Tom Tatarian recalls this account:

"They wheeled the big planes from the hangar and set up a makeshift, elevated stage, and the Glenn Miller Orchestra broke out with "In the Mood," and there was thunderous applause. The entire 398th Heavy Bomber Group attended. There must have been a thousand guys overall. There were no seats, so we all stood up and cheered that great band on. Johnny Desmond and the Crew Chiefs sang 'Chattanooga Choo Choo' just like the record that was so famous at the time. It was being home. Hearing 'In the Mood' and those other great tunes felt so good.

"We were all very young, mostly in our low twenties, and some guys were still teenagers. It was such an enjoyable evening that lasted about two hours. I was a tech-sargent at that time."

Tom was a typical G.I. who benefited by Glenn's great orchestra performances all over England. A bombadier, flight engineer, and a tailgunner, with over thirty missions accomplished. Tom Tatarian retired years later as Lt. Colonel.

Player List 1944

The American Band of the Allied Expeditionery Force

Conducted by Major Glenn Miller:

Trumpets: Master Sgt. Zeke Zarchy (lead and occasional solos); Sgt. Bernie Privin (most of the jazz solos); Sgt. Bobby Nichols (also soloist); Sgt. Whitey Thomas; Pfc. Jack Steele.

Trombones: Staff Sgt. Jimmy Priddy (lead) ; Sgt. John Halliburton; Pfc. Larry Hall; Pfc Nat Peck.

Saxophones: Sgt. Hank Freeman (lead alto and alto solos); Sgt. Peanuts Hucko (alto, tenor; clarinet solos); Sgt. Vince Carbone (tenor, and tenor solos); Cpl. Jack Ferrier (tenor, and tenor solos); Cpl. Freddy Guerra (alto); Pfc. Manny Thaler (baritone, alto, bass clarinet, occasional baritone solos; all doubled clarinets)

French Horn: Cpl. Addison Collins jr. (occasional solos) Violins: Staff Sgt. George Ockner (lead, and soloists); Staff Sgt. Harry Katzman (deputy leader); S/Sgt. Carl Swanson; Sgt. Dave Herman; Sgt. Dave Sackson; Cpl. Eugene Bergen; Cpl. Phil Cogliano (jazz solos); Cpl. Earl Cornwell; Cpl. Milton Edelson; Cpl. Nathan Kaproff; Cpl. Ernest Kardos; Cpl. Richard Motylinski; Pfc Joseph Kowalewski; Pfc Freddy Ostrovsky.

Violas: Sgt. Dave Schwartz; Sgt. Emanuel Wishnow; Cpl. Henry Brynan; Cpl. Stanley Harris.

Cellos: Cpl. Maurice Bialkin; Cpl. Bob Ripley.

Piano: Sgt. Mel Powell.

Guitar: Sgt. Carmen Mastren

Bass: Staff Sgt. Trigger Alpert

Drums: Technical Sgt. Ray McKinley

Reliefs: Pfc.Jack Russin (piano); Cpl. Joe Shulman (bass); Pfc Frank Ippolito (drums) Singer: Sgt. Johnny Desmond; Crew Chiefs singing group: Sgt. Steve Steck; Cpl. Murray Kane; Cpl. Artie Malvin; Pfc. Lynn Allison; Pfc. Gene Steck.

Arrangers: Tech Sgt. Jerry Gray; Master Sgt. Norman Leyden; Staff Sgt. Ralph Wilkinson.

Glenn, flanked by Paul Dudley and
Don Haynes - Dec. 12, 1944
(courtesy Army Air Force)

Missing Air Crew Report

WAR DEPARTMENT
HEADQUARTERS ARMY AIR FORCES
WASHINGTON
MISSING AIR CREW REPORT

1. ORGANIZATION: Location by Name: *Abbotts Ripton;* Command or Air Force: *VIII Air Force SVC;*
   Group: *35th ADG;* Squadron: *Repair;* Detachment: *2d Strategic Air Depot*
2. SPECIFY: Place of Departure: *Abbotts Ripton;* Course: BORDEAUX VIA A-42
   Target or Intended Destination: *Bordeaux A-42;* Type of Mission: *A*
3. WEATHER CONDITIONS AND VISIBILITY AT TIME OF CRASH OR WHEN LAST REPORTED:
   Unknown:
   GIVE: (a) Day: *15* Month: *December* Year: *44;* Time: *1355;* and Location: *Twinwood*
   of last known whereabouts of missing aircraft.
   (b) Specify whether aircraft was last sighted ( );
   Information not Available ( )
5. AIRCRAFT WAS LOST, OR IS BELIEVED TO HAVE BEEN LOST, AS A RESULT OF: (Check only
   one) Enemy Aircraft ( ); Enemy Anti-Aircraft ( ); Other Circumstances as Follows: *Unknown*
6. AIRCRAFT: Type, Model and Series: *UC-64A;* AAF Serial Number: *44-70285*
7. NICKNAME OF AIRCRAFT: If Any: *Norseman*
8. ENGINES: Type, Model and Series: *Radial – 1340 P & W;* AAF Serial Number:
   (a) *Unknown;* (b) (c) (d)
9. INSTALLED WEAPONS: (Furnish below Make, Type and Serial Number): *None*
10. THE PERSONS LISTED BELOW WERE REPORTED AS:
    Battle Casualty
11. NUMBER OF PERSONS ABOARD AIRCRAFT: Crew *1;* Passengers *2;* Total *3.*
    (Starting with Pilot, furnish the following particulars: If more than 11 persons were aboard aircraft, list
    similar particulars on separate sheet and attach original to this form).

Crew Position	Name in Full (Last Name First)	Rank	Serial Number	Current Status
1. Pilot	*Morgan, John R. S.*	*F/O*	*T-190776*	*Missing, AC*
2. Passenger	*Bassell, Norman F.*	*Lt Col*	*0-905387*	*Missing, AC*
3. Passenger	*Miller, Alton, G.*	*Major*	*0-50273*	*Missing, AC*

12. IDENTIFY BELOW THOSE PERSONS WHO ARE BELIEVED TO HAVE LAST KNOWLEDGE
    OF AIRCRAFT, AND CHECK APPROPRIATE COLUMN TO INDICATE BASIS FOR SAME.

Name in Full (Last Name First)	Rank	Serial Number	Contacted by Radio	Last Sighted	Saw Crash	Saw Forced Landing
1. *Unknown*						

13. IF PERSONNEL ARE BELIEVED TO HAVE SURVIVED, ANSWER YES TO ONE OF THE
    FOLLOWING STATEMENTS: (a) Parachutes were used ; (b) Persons were seen
    walking away from scene of crash.
14. ATTACH AERIAL PHOTOGRAPH, MAP, CHART, OR SKETCH, SHOWING APPROXIMATE
    LOCATION WHERE AIRCRAFT WAS LAST SEEN OR HEARD FROM.
15. ATTACH EYEWITNESS DESCRIPTION OF CRASH, FORCED LANDING, OR OTHER
    CIRCUMSTANCES PERTAINING TO MISSING AIRCRAFT.
16. GIVE NAME, RANK AND SERIAL NUMBER OF OFFICER IN CHARGE OF SEARCH, IF ANY,
    INCLUDING DESCRIPTION AND EXTEND: *None*

    For the Commanding Officer:

    Date of Report: *23 December 1944*

    (Signature of Preparing Officer)

17. REMARKS OR EYEWITNESS STATEMENTS: *None* RALPH S. CRAMER
    CAPT. A.C.
    ADJUTANT

MISSING IN FLIGHT
The Dudley Report

A DETAILED ACCOUNT OF MAJOR GLENN MILLER'S DISAPPEARANCE

By PAUL DUDLEY

As it appeared in Esquire Magazine's Year Book of the Jazz Scene 1947.

Bomblight Serenade

> *Paul Dudley, radio producer of the original Spotlight Band series for the Coca-Cola Company, was Glenn Miller's friend. As Technical Sergeant, he went overseas to write and direct all radio shows for the American Band of the Allied Expeditionery Force. Then as a newly appointed Warrant Officer JG, became operations officer for the entire unit and staged all broadcasts and personal appearances for the band while they were in England.*

"At 1:45 on the afternoon of December 15, 1944, Lt. Don Haynes drove Major Miller and Lt. Col. Norman Baesell to Twin Woods Farm RAF Mosquito Base near Bedford. As their car halted in front of the control tower, a plane swooped out of the heavy overcast, groped its way onto the runway and taxied over to pick up its passengers. "The following facts are listed to belie the fictions of the many rumor-happy gossipers who have erroneously reported the details surrounding Major Miller's departure: For those whose carelessly flapping tongues have reported that they witnessed Glenn taking off that day in a twin-engine Douglas C-47, it was actually a single-engine Norseman C-64, an all-metal plane equipped with one-way radio, fixed landing gear and a reputation of treachery in bad weather. For those badly informed 'experts' who claim that Miller was flying without orders, he was proceeding under an official order issued by SHAEF (Rear) to travel via Military Aircraft to the Continent on or about December 15. For the hundreds of others whose adventuresome imaginations have claimed that they were supposed to have been on the same plane, it was a seven passenger ship. It was flown by a pilot who had completed a lengthy tour of combat missions, Flight Officer Johnny Morgan. Lt. Haynes heard Glenn ask, "Where are the parachutes?" Then, Baesell's bluff reply, 'What the hell, Miller, do you want to live forever?'

"The ugly duckling airplane roared down the runway and its massive engine hauled it up into nowhere. For three days, the air above England was more ocean than sky. Then, the weather hung out its clouds to fly and an anxious band, sixty-two musicians, eager to take their first swing at Paris, piled into the C-47's, ready for almost anything, but the shock which awaited them. Orly Airfield was a welter of mud and confusion.

"Haynes, anticipating a detailed order from Glenn, checked the Operations Office for a message. Finding no word there, he called SHAEF (Forward) to discover that the Major had not checked in. Worried, he called the Paris Billeting Office. No quartering orders had been issued to Major Glenn Miller. By midnight, the band was bedded down at Hotel Des Olympiades, 22 Square Clignancourt in the Montmarte. Haynes and I walked and talked our way through the rest of the night combing hotels, bars and officer's clubs for a clue which would indicate that Major Miller had arrived safely in France. "Our hearts started to freeze with the fear that Glenn hadn't made it. We followed a breakfast of Red Cross coffee with a cross-channel call to a close friend and distant relative of the Major's, Operations Chief of the Eighth Air Force, General Orville Anderson. The shaggy taskmaster of America's big European bombing team went to work checking every inch of territory in England and France for the missing C-64. The General called us back seventy-two hours later to report, 'No dice. But we'll keep on trying.'

"On Christmas morning, we gathered the men in the front rows of the cold, dark Olympia Theater and Lt. Haynes pushed a few words over the lump in his throat to tell them that their Commanding Officer had been officially declared 'missing in flight'"

As Paul Dudley observed back in 1947, "Men like Glenn Miller don't just die. He will live musically for a long, long time. And, Glenn will live forever as a great friend in the hearts of the three million Yanks with whom he served overseas. He carried his quality wherever he went. As a civilian, his own personal and musical standards made him America's top band leader. In the Army, it made him the kind of leader men kept following after he was gone."

With an ability to sanctify musical perfection with vitality as he could crush imperfection that appeared in his ranks, Glenn Miller considered his musical offerings seriously, but with a soft heart lurking beyond his countenance.

"One night with bombs dropping on London and as I tried to elude fear and escape to the peace of sleep, Glenn was in the bed across the blackened room. Through the dark came his typical, tightlipped voice paraphrasing the 'hello, little friend' with which bomber pilots greeted their fighter escort in a rendezvous over enemy territory. 'Good night, little friend,' said Glenn.

"I felt reassured and closer to home, just as all the G.I.'s felt when they heard from Glenn Miller, and said, proudly as I say now,'Good night, Big friend.'"

THE GLENN MILLER MYSTIQUE
The Whole Nation Lost
When the Major Went Down

> *"We are still searching and hoping."*
> —Don Haynes, Glenn Miller's manager and friend,
> December 17, 1944.

The Glenn Miller mystique carries on year after year. Speculations about his disappearance surface from time to time. Some very silly, yet very interesting, if not Elvis-like speculations, have persisted.

According to Herb Caen of the "Stars and Stripes," Glenn's death was an assumption that some devotees found too grievous to bear. There were rumors of Glenn's survival, and many odd stories, some with little foundation and some with witnesses swearing that he survived.

Some say Glenn had a "date with lurking death." His closest friends disclosed that he had a premonition of his fate. Letters that he sent home shortly before his disappearance supposedly contained this note:

> *"I know I'm not coming back, but please don't worry. I couldn't have lived with myself if I hadn't come over here to do what little I can for these great guys."*

Just a few days before his last flight, Glenn received a letter from Helen that she had adopted a baby girl. It was said that upon receiving the news, Glenn went white. Beads of perspiration appeared on his forehead, and he muttered, "And I'll never see her."

And, Caen reported the following: "An ironic little scene was enacted at the airport where Glenn climbed into the small plane. Glancing around the inside of the plane, Glenn noted: 'Hey, there aren't any parachutes in here.' 'What's the matter, Miller?' asked the pilot, 'You wanna live forever.'"

Chris Valenti's files
Interesting Information and Reports

Dr. Chris Valenti of "The Big Band Broadcast" radio program, originating from Long Island's WHPC, 90.3 FM in Garden City, New York, regularly discusses this phenomenon with faithful listeners:

"The greatest mystery in entertainment history is the disappearance of Glenn Miller. On that date of destiny, December 15, 1944, the driver who took Miller to the plane on that tiny airfield reported that, on the plane, besides Glenn Miller, was pilot, Flight Officer John Morgan and Lt. Colonel Norman Baesell, who invited Glenn to join him in his personal flight to Paris. To add to some other odd information, the pilot who was ordered to search for Miller when the plane was reported late, says he firmly believes Miller was not on that plane at all. Some rumors persist reporting it was common knowledge that Miller was accidentally shot by an M.P. in Paris within days after his arrival; one of them reporting they actually saw the news report when it came off a military teletype. Others swear they saw Miller's body being brought down on a stretcher after being shot by a jealous husband in Germany. It was also reported that Miller had died in the arms of a prostitute in a Paris brothel. Then, there is the even odder claim by some that Miller died of wounds in Ohio, as was thought, documented by the New Jersey State Health Department, but was later rescinded. Glenn had lived in New Jersey at the time of his disappearance.

So, after 60 years, the incredible Miller mystique lingers on.

Chris Valenti
(courtesy C. Valenti)

"I started this investigation on Glenn Miller under the Freedom of Information Act," continued Dr. Valenti, "receiving numerous calls and letters, and basic responses. But, six months into the investigation I mentioned on the air about the Ohio story. As a result I received a letter from one of the attending physicians who attended to Glenn Miller in Ohio, as well as threats not to repeat the story on the air, by some unknown male person."

The threats by the anonymous caller never materialized, although Valenti surrounded himself with hired security at the studio, enhanced by volunteer fans who were worried about the popular disc jockey.

It was military driver Edward McCollough who drove Glenn to Twinwood Farm airfield, where a C-64 single engine airplane, named the Norseman, was waiting to take Glenn to Paris. He was with Glenn the night before:

"I told him I was assigned by my commanding officer to take him around that evening, and the next morning to the airfield.

"We met and shook hands, and I told him I was pleased to meet him. He asked me to take him to the NCO club (Non-commissioned Officers) and not to the officers club because they were stuffed shirts.

The Next morning, which was December 15th, I picked him up a little later than planned, because foggy conditions prevented a take off.

It was about 9:00 AM when we arrived at Twinwood. The pilot, Flight Officer Morgan, came out to greet Miller. There was no one else on that plane that I could see. I remained until the plane took off. I had stayed outside the plane and watched it take off. There was a very low overhead, so the plane disappeared out of sight rapidly. Put all other stories to rest. I saw him get on that plane and take off, never to return."

It was 34 degrees when the plane took off without de-icing equipment. Morgan was an accomplished pilot and had flown many missions in a B-24 bomber.

According to Dr. Valenti, other speculations were: "Arnold Smith, listener, and CW operator, now a "ham," was stationed in Paris when the call came over about the shooting at the Hotel DeParee. The military police were sitting at a pinochle card game when the call came."

Smith: "I rode in the Jeep to the scene and saw an accident of some kind. A body was brought down on a stretcher, and a civilian about 25 years old was led away in foot cuffs and hand cuffs. The next day somebody sent me a story from a Frankfurt, Germany newspaper, reporting that Glenn Miller died while with a prostitute in a Paris brothel."

There was a story attributed to a German reporter named Udo Ulfkotte, saying Miller died from a heart attack while in the arms of a prostitute and that the story was covered up because he was an important American personality and it would be damaging to the psychology of the war-effort. Dr. Valenti interviewed Mr. Ulfkotte by telephone, live and on the air. Ulfkotte totally denied the story. He was not surprised, however, that the story was linked to him. But, he assured Dr. Valenti that the story had since been classified as a rumor.

In a conversation with Mr. A.C. Griffith of Virginia, Dr. Valenti learned Griffith had talked to two believable witnesses, that it was common knowledge that Miller had been shot in Paris. Griffith said that Ed Schneider, an American Military Engineer, had received the teletype revealing the story and that he tore it off the machine and placed it on the commanding Colonel's desk. It reported that Miller had been shot in Paris. The next day the coverup of the lost plane story prevailed, reporting that perhaps bombs accidentally had been dropped on the Miller plane by English planes returning from an aborted sortie over Germany.

Then, there was the bizarre story that Colonel Baesell was involved in the black market and had shot Glenn and the pilot on the way to France, then landed the plane safely.

FINAL STATEMENT

The theory that bombs were dropped below landing on top of the single engine aircraft, blasting Miller's plane out of the sky over the English Channel has some validity according to an Associated Press release in 1999. Theory: the plane was blasted out of the sky by 4000 lb. bombs jettisoned by a Royal Air Force squadron returning from Siegen, Germany, following an aborted raid.

The bombs were let loose from the bombers, because they could not land with the bombs aboard. An entry in a military logbook confirmed that the aborted raid occurred on the same day as Miller's disappearance, with no trace ever found of the plane or its passengers. The single engine plane was flying low, just above the waterline. Royal Air Force navigator Fred Shaw, recalls seeing a small plane spiraling out of control after the bombs were dropped, and watched it disappear into the Channel.

The other most accepted theory: That bad judgment was responsible. That a Colonel, anxious to get to Paris, and an adventuresome pilot taking off in unacceptable weather conditions, allowed the plane to ice up, or, the fog grounding and blinding them into the Channel, are the most likely, haunting theories of the historic mystery of the loss of Major Glenn Miller, the most popular bandleader of the era of the big bands. Dr. Valenti declares in his investigation that the above statements are, at last, the probable truth, and he has finally put the investigation to rest forever.

If Major Glenn Miller hadn't disappeared, what musical road would he have taken at war's end upon returning home to resume his life with his world-famous group of fine, now seasoned musicians?

Glenn harbored many tricks up his sleeve, always being psychologically prepared in the event of failure of any one

---

of his music ventures. After his first band failed, he charted his second, and just before the opening, stated: "Well, Glen Island will be the acid test (for the newly formed band). If we don't make it this time, I'm going back to Denver to open a garage."

A day later the garage business was placed on permanent hold. The so-called acid test had passed with honors. Another idea once occurred to Glenn, according to his manager and friend Don Haynes: "Glenn thought about opening a chain of motels just for the traveling bands, or forming an orchestra with strings, and always had hoped that if his next band was successful, he would limit his touring with the band to six months a year and spend the other half year at home with his wife and children."

Glenn had purchased a ranch he named "Tuxedo Junction" in Monrovia, California. He figured to do some salmon fishing in the Columbia River and raise oranges at the ranch, and do an occasional recording date. Plans like this were discussed between Don Haynes and Glenn the night of December 14, 1944.

In an interview with Woody Herman in 1982, we talked about Glenn Miller's prevailing style:

"If Glenn had returned from Europe, by now he would be playing something different, and not the usual charts. Like all of us leaders, including Miller, Artie Shaw, whoever, our next record is our favorite and the recordings of our

R. Grudens and Woody Herman
Southampton - 1982

past are exactly that—recordings of the past—music history. Even Glenn would have found it boring to play the same charts over and over. There are things I have been very proud of that were good for its time. But, a band must move on musically, or it will die, although, I must admit the Glenn Miller recordings live on and are constantly selling year after year. They were universal recordings that people always will enjoy. Who knows. Music constantly changes, and that's one gratifying thing about the whole scene. Today's music is completely different from the music of the forties. And tomorrow's music will be different than today's. You can be sure."

On December 18, 1945, the U.S. Army declared Major Glenn Miller "Officially Dead."

Glenn Receives the Bronze Star
1945

In 1945, Glenn Miller Received the recognitions he justly deserved, The Bronze Star, bestowed upon Mrs. Helen Miller by Colonel F.R. Kerr:

For meritorious service in connection with military operations as Commander of the Army Air Force Band (Special), from 9 July 1944 to 15 December 1944. Major Miller, through excellent judgment and professional skill, conspicuously blended the abilities of the outstanding musicians, comprising the group, into a harmonious orchestra whose noteworthy contribution to the morale of the armed forces has been little less than sensational. Major Miller constantly sought to increase the services rendered by his organization, and it was through him that the band was ordered to give this excellent entertainment to as many troops as possible. His superior accomplishments are highly commendable and reflect the highest credit upon himself and the armed forces of the United States.

The Glenn Miller Festival
at Twinwood Airport - 2003

Sixty Years Later at Twinwood

Memories of the Royal Air Force Twinwood Airfield Control Tower, a new museum and a Celebration.

During World War II, Twinwood Airfield was used as a training base, and a satellite for nearby Cranfield Airfield. It was an RAF base, but both British and American aircraft used it.

Many entertainers, including Bob Hope, Bing Crosby and Glenn Miller, used Twinwood to fly throughout the country on their numerous concert tours.

On that foggy day December 15, 1944, Glenn Miller waited in the control tower before he boarded a Norseman Aircraft bound for Paris. As we know, he was never seen again.

One day in 2000, singer Beryl Davis was filming a video for her theme song, "I'll Be Seeing You," with a BBC producer and a cameraman, when they ran into the owners of the then defunct tower. When the owners realized the buildings' history and its ties to the Glenn Miller disappearance mystique, they moved to restore the site. Twinwood Events restored the control tower and it is now open to the public to explore and experience.

The unique atmosphere of this historic building contains a superb museum dedicated to Glenn, an RAF room dedicated to the RAF personnel stationed there and a gallery of wartime aviation art. You step back in time as you ascend the stairway to experience the unforgettable World War II RAF tower. Once there you may purchase music, books, magazines, souvenirs and refreshments.

During August of 2003, vocalist Beryl Davis returned to Twinwood to sing with Ray McVay and the entire Glenn Miller Orchestra UK, a direct franchise of Glenn Miller Productions of Florida,USA.

Twinwood Airfield & Control Tower

THE GLENN MILLER MUSEUM

Twinwood Arena

It was followed by performances of the Bill Baker Big Band, The Mainline Band, The Classic Swing Band, and The Tony Strudwick Band, and featured the unforgettable music of Glenn Miller.

The historical event will continue annually into the future, for as long as Glenn Miller's music is heard.

Beryl Davis and Boys of the RAF at Twinwood

Tex Beneke Directs his own Band in 1946
(courtesy Tex Beneke)

PART THREE

THE MUSICIANS, VOCALISTS, ARRANGERS AND LEADERS WHO SHARED THE BANDSTAND SPEAK OUT

The Chesterfield broadcasts "On the Air"

Tex Beneke

A December 1, 1997 Interview and Beyond

It was always enjoyable talking with Gordon "Tex" Beneke, as we did from time to time. The Texas drawl was comfortably familiar. The sound of his voice, spoken or in song, defined, for me, the personality of the Glenn Miller Orchestra, especially when vocalizing tunes like "Chattanooga Choo-Choo," "I've Got a Gal in Kalamazoo,"

Marion Hutton, Glenn and Tex Beneke
(R. Grudens collection)

"Jukebox Saturday Night," "Don't Sit Under the Apple Tree," and those charming conversations when setting up selected tunes on some memorable Glenn Miller evergreens. True, Tex is not what you would define as a bona fide vocalist, and he did not desire to become one, but Glenn Miller drafted him. Tex was trying to please his new boss, so he went along with it.

> *"You sure can play the tenor, all right, Texas,"* he said to his newest sax player, *"but we need you for some vocals too,"* Tex Beneke explained. *"At first I wasn't sure what he meant."*

Although we had conversed many times, Tex had been facing some ongoing health problems, the discomfort restricting his activities. I found him snuggled up at home with his wife, Sandi, and we were able to enjoy a long conversation about his favorite subject, the vastly celebrated Glenn Miller Orchestra, and his own inimitable contributions to that legendary musical organization.

On various Miller recording's you could hear Glenn or the Modernaires singing group vamp with words as Tex, whistling, worked himself down from the sax section to the mike in front of the bandstand where he would take up the vocal.

"Hi there, Tex, what'cha say?" Paula Kelly and the Modernaires would chant, and Tex Beneke replied, singing: **"Step aside, partner, it's my day. Lend an ear and listen to my version,"** and the Modernaires added, **"of a really solid Tennessee excursion..."** And, you know the rest. It's the opening lines to the very first Gold Record, the immortal "Chattanooga Choo Choo," for which this book is named. Oh, how wonderful it is to hear that 1941 recording spin on the old turntable time after time after time. I never get tired of playing it. So many Glenn Miller/Tex Beneke fans feel the same way.

Gordon Beneke was born in Fort Worth, Texas in 1914. Playing sax since he was nine years old, he began playing in local territory bands. Gordon joined the Ben Young Band and toured from Texas to Ohio.

"In Detroit, I got this call from a guy by the name of Glenn Miller. I didn't know who he was at the time. He was starting a new band, and Gene Krupa recommended me because he had heard me in Young's band one night when he was scouting local bands for personnel for his band. Glenn wanted to know if I was interested. He flat out offered me $50.00 a week, the same as everybody would be making to start, and promised to build on from there. I hesitated, then asked him for $52.50 so I could be the highest paid member. Dead silence—Glenn was frugal, you know—'O.K.,' he said, 'but you'll have to prove yourself.'"

Gordon Beneke drove his 1936 Plymouth for twenty-four hours through inclement snow to his first rehearsal.

"When it came time for me to take a vocal on a song called 'Doin' the Jive'—Glenn sang 'Hi, there Tex, what'cha say?' That's when the whole business of calling me 'Tex' began. I guess he liked that Texas drawl. Now, only people from my old home town ever call me Gordon.

"I was just a green-horn kid sitting there in the sax section, nothing but a sideman, strictly. All I wanted was my money. I didn't care what he recorded. It didn't matter to me. I knew we were going to do some records this day. I wanted to hear myself back too, for I had never heard myself before...in the beginning, you know. But, it didn't matter to me. All I wanted was my record check so I could get it to the bank in a hurry."

After a favorable beginning at the Glen Island Casino in New Rochelle, New York, the second Glenn Miller Orchestra began a national tour. "We were all young and didn't mind traveling," Tex said, "People would come from hundreds of miles away to hear us play. We'd perform at theaters, barns, parks, dance halls, and dance pavilions. We didn't know we were making history. We were just enjoying ourselves and making a living."

Ray Eberle, Glenn, Marion and Tex
(R. Grudens collection)

Tex Beneke quickly became a valuable commercial personality for Glenn's band. Glenn never missed an opportunity to feature Tex playing and vocalizing on specialty tunes. Tex was always cast into the spotlight and the public loved him. He found it difficult to learn lyrics but could learn anything on the sax if he heard it just once.

"It's ironic, Richard," Tex continued, "I really didn't like most of those tunes I sang including 'Chattanooga Choo-Choo.' All I was interested in was playing my sax. Of course, I had to go along with the vocal in order to be accepted. I had to do what Glenn wanted. That was part of the deal. Finally he put me doing parts with the Modernaires."

Tex was destined to become a different kind of a singer, something I call a non-singer, much like Louis Armstrong is a singing non-singer. He first thought "Chattanooga Choo Choo" was a dog and would not get off the ground: "But every time we played and sang it, the roof would come off the place. I really didn't care about singing. All I considered myself to be was a poor man's Johnny Mercer. I always steer clear of it until I have to sing on some of the jobs when I'm leading my own orchestra. The folks want to hear those favorites, you know. I had to keep some of those arrangements to please the folks, especially the ones that made it big.

"Anything we did at these shows or dance parties were very well received. At that time, everybody was band-conscious. The bands got on coast-to-coast radio shows that made them famous overnight. Wherever we appeared, the people were drawn to us, they had to see us in-person.

Tex and his fellow musicians were not always enamored of playing Glenn Miller material.

"Our band was precise, but some of us yearned to play Charlie Barnet kind of stuff, if you know what I mean. We couldn't wait for our sessions to end so we could sit in with real swinging bands that were in town, bands that were more jazzy and more interesting for us to experience. As soon as we could get off the bandstand. and there was some other band playing nearby that we dug, we were flying."

Notes before a recording session:

Frank Dailey's Meadowbrook in New Jersey

The band was playing over at Frank Dailey's in the Meadowbrook. So the night before they had gone through and played all the things needed for the daily recording. Glenn said "So fellows, I'm going to leave it up to you to put your own parts in your own cases and bring your own things with you in the morning. Don't forget!" Tex promptly put all his materials back in the book, folded it up, packed it away, went home, went to bed, got up the next morning, went to the record station, and everybody had their music material but Tex.

"I don't have a part bag—see. Everything was set, the engineers were set and the air time was bought. Now, because I forgot my stuff, Glenn had to call off the session. Boy, was Glenn pretty rough with me for a few days. That's the first and last time anything like that would ever happen to me again."

Glenn relied a lot on Tex Beneke. Helping in the sax section, and trying to iron out something that wasn't just exactly right. "Especially where the phrasing was concerned or where to mark the breathers, we could play six bars or eight bars, and then, depending on the tempo of the tune. Glenn used to call on me to do a lot of solos. He always liked to look at the guys when they played, and especially me, because I was in the front row. He would put his eye on Johnny Best and he would stare at him, with his glasses down on his nose, like a freeze, and Johnny would come off the mike shaking like a leaf. He used to say the old man put the fish eye on him. He'd come over to me and say, 'OK Texas, let me hear you blow now.'"

"I'd stand up and start playing, he would stare at me and I would stare back at him. At the end of a chorus, he'd say, 'Take another one of them, Texas, they're small.' And sometimes he would have me blowing 20 or 30 choruses. I would be flat out by that time and almost collapse, the other guys couldn't understand how I could stand up there and play and glare at Glenn and have Glenn glare back at me. But, Glenn got a charge out of that. I wasn't afraid of him like some of the others guys were. Not really afraid of him, but he could really make you nervous."

Like many others, Gordon "Tex" Beneke invoked a vocal opinion of his much revered boss:

"I thought Glenn was great, but he lacked a lot when it came to being a fine, jazz trombone player. He could play fair dixieland material, as is proven earlier in his career on many of the old recordings with countless other bands. He was a good lead trombone player and a good section man. He would leave most of the jazz, and stuff like that, to some of the other fellows. He had—oh, I don't know what it was, he could tell anybody, even though he only played trombone, he could teach you on your own instrument, no matter what it was, and make you an accomplished player. He taught me so much about saxophone and he did the same with all the other guys.

> *According to George Simon, author of the definitive book, Glenn Miller and His Orchestra, band members always thought that Tex Beneke was a gentleman and a generous friend to everyone, adding warmth and wholesomeness to the band.*

A short while after Glenn's disappearance over the English Channel in 1944, Tex took over the band. "I was asked by Mrs. (Helen) Miller if I would front the Army Air Force Band in 1946. I did and we broke the record at the Hollywood Palladium in 1947. We had 6,750 people dancing on opening night. The Glenn Miller name was just magic.

TEX BENEKE

6/01/98

Hi, Richard:

Thank you so very much for sending me a copy of
"THE MUSIC MEN" - - - Sorry I haven't gotten back
to you long before now, but I've been feeling so
lousy the past few months, I just haven't been
able to correspond with anyone!   The guy who
said "THESE ARE THE GOLDEN YEARS" had ROCKS in
his head!   Afraid I'm now going thru all the
infirmities of my age-bracket . . and can't do
anything about it!!

What I've read so far, Richard, is great and I'll
try to get the questionaire off to you soon as
possible.   It's a kick reading about so many of
my personal friends of long ago.   Certainly brings
back many wonderful memories!

Gotta go now, Richard (time for my pills) but
will try to do better next time.

Sincerely,

Tex

A letter from Tex
(R. Grudens collection)

I kept the job until 1950, when I decided to form my own band. I called it the Tex Beneke Orchestra. We played to capacity audiences everywhere. In New York, we played the Paramount, the Pennsylvania Hotel and performed in lots of shows in Disneyland, California. We called our music *The Music Made Famous By Glenn Miller* and played right into the 1980's."

Tex and his band had played through 1997. My friend, Patty Andrews, of the famed Andrews Sisters singing group was a frequent guest as were some other original Miller personnel, including vocalist Ray Eberle and the then current version of the Modernaires.

"I always found it comfortable singing with Tex and his guys," Patty Andrews told me recently. "We played with Glenn Miller's original civilian orchestra on the Chesterfield programs way back when, and we always had a good time singing all those great songs with Glenn."

Final words of that 1997 interview with Tex:

"Today, Richard, we do engagements mostly at private parties, which are not open to the public. Sometimes at the Elk's Club or at night clubs and theaters. Looking back—all I can ever think about—that special place in my heart—is that the Glenn Miller Orchestra itself was the highlight of my career. Just to be able to work with a man like Glenn, somebody who knew exactly what he wanted and worked hard enough to get it. He was a fine arranger, a good lead trombone player, and an excellent person, someone to look up to always. He also made a singer out of me—that was something in itself."

Paul Tanner

During the summer of 1938, Glenn Miller found a skinny, stammering kid named Paul Tanner playing trombone in the Swing Club, an Atlantic City strip club he visited one night after completing his own performance. Glenn and Helen thought they were night-clubbing, until the show began. When Paul learned that Glenn was in the house, he mustered up enough courage to approach Glenn for an opinion of his playing. The two became engrossed in conversation that led to Paul being invited by Glenn to join his band right there on the spot.

One of six boys, Paul Tanner came from Skunk Hollow, Kentucky. The family moved to Wilmington, Delaware, where his dad was superintendent of a state reformatory for boys. Aided by a few trombone playing inmates, Paul Tanner mastered the trombone by the time he completed high school. He otherwise moved very slowly. Glenn facetiously named him Lightnin'. Paul had been playing part-time with Marty Caruso's band after short innings with Frank Dailey's famed Meadowbrook Ballroom band in New Jersey.

"The guys in Caruso's band liked my playing, so they chipped in and hired me for $15.00 a week out of their own pocket. I was ambitious, but pretty scared. When I finally got up the nerve to talk to Glenn that night, I stammered like mad.

"I said: 'If you like my p-playing, would you give me a recommendation? But, he had other ideas for me, saying, 'How soon can you pack up and go with me and my band?' And I said, "'This is all I've got,' pointing to my trombone. 'I'm ready right now.' And so I went with the band. It lasted four glorious years that moved me to say one day, that when I was with the Glenn Miller Orchestra, every night was like New Year's Eve."

An accomplished upper register player when Paul first joined the band, Glenn decided to assign him only lower register parts because he wanted more of an all-around player rather than a specialist. Paul Tanner listened to Glenn who turned out to be right.

In an interview with L.A. Jazz Scene Magazine, writer John Tumpak, Paul Tanner explained:

"One of the first things I learned about Glenn was that he was willing to work brutally hard to achieve perfection.

"He was an extremely knowledgeable musician, an astute businessman, a great organizer, a chronic workaholic, and extremely patriotic. He made me an even better player. And, he was a very fine and underrated trombone player himself.

"He had good tone, a respectable upper range, and was very consistent. He could also arrange and was a very good editor. I remember him spending hours on an entire score to achieve the sound standard he wanted. A good example is how he rewrote Joe Garland's 'In the Mood' to turn it into a huge hit. And take 'Slip Horn Jive' for example. It was he and I playing the trombone solos. It was a very precise number and you simply didn't make errors. If there were problems in the saxophone section, something Glenn didn't understand about brass, he would simply rearrange the chart, but, if there was a note missed on a trombone, he understood and tolerated that. He understood if you missed a note, but if you came in wrong, he didn't understand that, and guys were fired for too much of that. When it came to reed problems on other brass, he never understood that, either. To Glenn there were mistakes, and there were mistakes.

"On the recording 'Slip Horn Drive,' it was Glenn and me on the trombone. Glenn's trombone solo was very good, and Glenn was a good trombone player.

At Carnegie Hall on October 6, 1939, Paul remembers the band being a little tense. It was a place they had always heard about. For all of them in the band, it was extremely prestigious to be invited to appear on the revered stage, which musicians of the time regarded with great awe.

"Jerry Gray wrote the arrangement of 'Tuxedo Junction.' Glenn was a very smart musician and he always seemed to know exactly what he wanted. There was never any communication problem unless someone tried to cross him. Then you were off to the guillotine. As far as explaining things musically, this was never a problem. Speaking about how the band would advance, listen to something as simple as 'Tuxedo Junction.' If I remember it right, we took the arrangement that was given to us, then we rehearsed all night long, like six or seven hours, just to put that thing finally into shape."

"Those great recordings that the orchestra performed was headed by one man, Glenn Miller! He was the head man, and nothing went on that he didn't O.K. He ran the whole thing and that was that. Maybe that's why it all worked so well and has lasted so long. There was only one leader and it was not a case of too many cooks, if you know what I mean!

"I learned a lot from Glenn's playing and so did the other fellows. But, Glenn cut back his playing because he didn't want to be compared to Tommy and feel competitive. It was easier to cut back and let the guys in the band do their job."

According to Paul Tanner, after "Chattanooga," the band was swinging more for several reasons. One, Glenn wasn't quite so worried about money like he was before his great success. Glenn became more relaxed:

Paul Tanner: "And, very frankly, we all knew that we were going into the service. It wasn't like today when kids don't know, and they have it hanging over them. We all knew. There was no question. If you could walk around, you were going in. We lost the fear of losing our jobs, and so the band started to swing more, and it was a beautiful thing. Some of the very latest records that we made actually swing much more than the band that was on the way to becoming so famous. So, eight days after 'Chattanooga,' we recorded a great swinging version of 'Don't Sit Under the Apple Tree.'"

THE TROMBONE SECTION

Jimmy Priddy   Frank D'Anolfo

Paul Tanner   Glenn Miller

At the Hotel Pennsylvania, Paul tells about the afternoon shows for teenagers in the Cafe Rouge. The people were charged twenty-five cents to get in. The kids would just sit down and milk a coke or perhaps dance. Glenn was happy to support the special attention during those appearances, but the waiters were not happy. Glenn would give away one radio-phonograph, along with a stack of records, to a military base, and apparently not just Glenn Miller records. And, Paul went on, "Glenn paid for the prize out of his own pocket."

Big Band Jump Newsletter once asked Paul Tanner if he thought the ability to play music is principally genetic. "As a music professor, I've heard that often, but I am not convinced of it because there were six brothers in our family, three of them were able to play professionally and three couldn't.

The three that played professionally practiced a lot.

It's a situation of a work ethic, and we got nothing but encouragement at home, but I think a couple of the brothers who didn't play professionally wanted to start at the top and didn't want to build up muscles and all that sort of thing, but I don't know if genes have anything to do with it."

When Glenn's band played their last performance on September 27, 1942, at the Central Theater in Passaic, New Jersey, just before Glenn joined the U.S. Army to organize a military big band, the mood was weepy. Marion Hutton choked up and had to leave the stage. The Modernaires could not complete their number, and some kids in the crowd were actually sobbing. Realizing the futility of continuing, Glenn had the curtain brought down. According to Paul Tanner, "It was the end of an era."

Paul Tanner filled the years following playing with Charlie Spivak, and spent some time in the Army, working G.I. radio shows, films, and playing trombone on those big band wartime "V" discs, recorded exclusively for the troops entertainment in war zones overseas. After the war, he played for a while with Les Brown's Band, eventually reuniting with fellow Miller alumnus Tex Beneke and his band for six additional, happy years. The University of California at Los Angeles drew Paul Tanner into its fold and within seven years his BA degree earned him a teaching position as Professor of Music. Over the years, he obtained his Masters and PhD. degrees. After teaching music to over seventy-five thousand students, writing 20 books on music theory and the trombone, and traveling as trombone soloist with the UCLA Concert Band in the off times, Paul Tanner retired from it all in 1981, after quite a marvelous musical life. When he retired, his students showcased a rare, but sizable party at the college that included an appearance of the entire Tex Beneke big band and some familiar Glenn Miller alumni and friends.

Paul Tanner had performed as a side man with Henry Mancini, Nelson Riddle, Neal Hefti, and Pete Rugolo, and in 1975 was a founder of the World Jazz Association. Today,

Paul Tanner regularly hits the cruise ship circuit, along with performers like the perennial Beryl Davis, another alumnus of the great, world famous Glenn Miller Orchestra.

Always a trombone player first, Paul Tanner is a much loved gracious professor second. And, for the record, Paul's favorite Glenn Miller tunes were their version of "Rhapsody in Blue," "Serenade in Blue," and "Spring Will Be a Little Late This Year." "I prefer those kind of tunes."

Tuxedo Junction
Words by
BUDDY FEYNE
Music by
ERSKINE HAWKINS
WILLIAM JOHNSON
JULIAN DASH
featured by
GLENN MILLER
and his ORCHESTRA

John Chalmers
"Chummy" MacGregor
Piano

On one November day in 1932, Glenn was introduced to piano player Chummy MacGregor at the Lowrey Hotel in St. Paul, Minnesota, where they both began work in Smith Ballew's band. Ballew's pianist, Fulton McGrath, had just been replaced by MacGregor.

In 1937, Glenn hired Chummy to play in his first band. A decent, loyal, devoted, but just above average piano player, Chummy MacGregor nurtured a solid friendship with Glenn Miller. He assisted Glenn in the business aspect of the band and occasionally as a driver when on tours. Along with jazz clarinetist Hal McIntyre, who also became a personal friend of Glenn's, the three spent off-bandstand time together, and both usually drove in a car with Glenn, rather than travel in

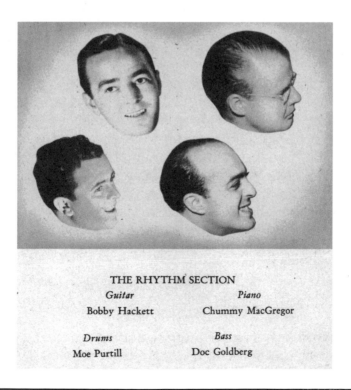

THE RHYTHM SECTION

Guitar	Piano
Bobby Hackett	Chummy MacGregor
Drums	*Bass*
Moe Purtill	Doc Goldberg

the band bus with the other musicians. The Glenn Miller Story portrayed the two as extremely close friends, which was not the case.

Finding a musical gem.

According to Chummy: "The band traveled by bus from the Glen Island Casino to the Victor Recording Studios in New York City almost every day. Because of our heavy schedule, the band required more material {to record} and we had to search everywhere for it. One day there was a kid stationed in front of the Plymouth hotel. He was offering big band scores to musicians for five bucks, and Glenn bought a few, like he always would. One was a chart written by Joe Garland, a trumpet player in Louis Armstrong's band.

Glenn and Chummy
(R. Grudens collection)

"Since he sold the scores to anybody, they weren't acceptable for our use in their original state. We had to fix them up to make them our own. On this particular piece, all we used of the original was the two front saxophone parts, and a few other parts in the middle. We threw in some solos and worked it up from then on out. I wrote the finishing coda twenty minutes before airtime at the Casino. This was on August 1st, 1939. We ran it down, brass and saxophone separately, on the balcony of the Casino between sets, then we put it right on the air.

"The piece was 'In the Mood.' I think you'll agree it was worth the five bucks. Of course the rest is history. The arrangement got softer and softer toward the end and then, wham! It sure was an attention getter—and it became an immediate hit. What mileage we got out of it, and am I ever sick of it. If I never have to hear it again, it would be okay with me."

Every time he looked up, Glenn's new orchestra found themselves on the air. Everyone was picking up on them—the great, new Glenn Miller Orchestra. They were recording all day, everyday, after shows and before shows, it was unbelievable. Then they worked all the night time radio programs, getting very little sleep and then they were back in the recording studio the next morning. Everyone worked like mad.

"We knew something big was happening to us. That summer of 1939 was a springboard for the band. But we really didn't feel the impact, but 16,000 people showed up at the State Fair in Auburn. A couple days later when we arrived at the New York Paramount, the lines went for blocks, from Broadway all the way to Eight Avenue and back. The kids had stayed up all night."

On April 4th, 1939 the band recorded four sides, "The Lady's in Love," "And the Angels Sing," "The Chestnut Tree," and most importantly, Glenn's own composition and theme, the beautiful and rich "Moonlight Serenade."

According to Chummy, the original version of "Moonlight Serenade" had never been arranged satisfactorily. It was keyed too high. Glenn had written it in G-Flat. For the opening theme it seemed okay, but when they finished the radio program and the trumpets were worn out, they had to face that relentless theme once again.

Chummy: "That high register was just too much. So, sometime previously, Glenn had re-scored it in a more civilized register, using the clarinet lead and the saxophone setup. And we had recorded it on our last Bluebird date. While the record was released, and of all things, started to break for a hit, we had to get the publisher to restrict radio performances by other artists to keep it from getting too big a play as this would spoil it as a theme song. I always thought it was a wonderful theme. I don't know why, but there seems to be a certain sadness about that song."

**It's Opening Night at the Glen Island Casino
and the band plays over a
Nationwide Radio Network Hookup.**

Chummy: "This was the tip-off for our great, future success. The Casino had the hippest playing bunch of waiters that I ever ran into. They would hang around at rehearsals. You'd think they had a piece of the action. Now, on the air, especially when the band was going on some jazz tune, they'd go into action, and were they ever for us. Trays were held high, hips rotating, fingers snapping, back and forth from their respective stations, they'd be playing like mad. They made you feel great. You felt like you were winning for sure."

When the program was finished the musicians in the band would lay down their instruments and head for coffee into the kitchen for a coffee break while Glenn discussed the program with NBC representatives. Almost immediately, the phone in back of the bandstand began to ring. Glenn received personal congratulations from fellow musicians and friends, bandleader Gene Krupa, Gil Rodin from the Bob Crosby band at the College Inn from Chicago, Jimmy Dorsey from California, Russ Morgan from someplace in Indiana, and Charlie Barnet from the Meadowbrook just across the Hudson, in New Jersey. Chummy: "All our good friends called just to say hello."

"A couple of nights before Christmas, we played a bunch of music at the Satellite Ballroom in Harlem against Erskine Hawkins and his band. It was great listening to them and their wonderful drive. Funny thing—we got the biggest ovation we had gotten anywhere. Incidentally, it was here that we picked up 'Tuxedo Junction' that was part of their book—but it was a much different version than the one we had cooked up."

One day, after a six side recording session at the RCA Victor Studios in New York, Chummy MacGregor recalls Glenn being too sick to join the opening of an engagement at the New York Paramount.

Chummy: "In February he had picked up an infection and stayed away for a couple of nights, but his condition steadily worsened. He went to his hotel room and in a couple of days he took a turn for the worse and they carried him off to the hospital in an ambulance. He looked terrible. I knew if Glenn could not walk out under his own steam, he was in pretty bad shape. On top of this we were due to open the next day at the Paramount theater for a return engagement. First show was at eight A.M. with the kids lined up all around the block.

"We decided that (Hal) McIntyre would lead the band onstage. He was always very outgoing and made friends everywhere. I called him Joe Rotary. Under the circumstances we thought he would do the most to front it, but, you know what, he was awful. Talk about stage fright, he was frozen with terror.

"The word got out on the street that Glenn was not there, so the usual kids that hung around the stage door dwindled to a handful. And, from noisy packed houses and kids dancing in the aisles to a two thirds capacity house. I didn't understand it."

The band never figured Glenn would be that important as an up-front leader. Everyone realized how important he was to the band, but he never sold himself to an audience, he just did what he was supposed to do with no flamboyancy or show business flare. Many bandleaders in those days performed antics of one kind or another while the band played. Glenn wanted none of that, and, lo and behold, people were staying away. Apparently, Glenn was the one they came to see:

"We just couldn't get over it. Something had to be done. So arrangements were made for other bandleaders to front the band each show—Charlie Barnet, Woody Herman, Tommy Dorsey, Russ Morgan, Gene Krupa, anyone who was in town took a turn at it. Somehow we got through the first week. Glenn returned the second week to sellout crowds ending with a gross of over 100,000 dollars.

"To everyone, the most lasting impression of Glenn was his wholesomeness. To all you mothers, I just hope your son grows up as intrinsically good and upright a man as he. Not that he was a moralist or a prude; far from it.

He certainly was no stuffed shirt, but in the highways and byways of the jazz scene, he stood out from the crowd like the Washington Monument.

"He just couldn't help it. So much class, such a good mind, good looks and such a healthy sense of humor."

To Chummy MacGregor, there seemed to be a certain sadness about Glenn's theme, "Moonlight Serenade:"

> *"Maybe its because of the tragic events that followed, but I get a lump in my throat every time I hear it played and I'm not alone in this either. Many, many times over the years since, I've seen a strange phenomenon take place. The various times when I had been visiting somewhere, it might be a large affair, or maybe just a small group, and in the course of the evening, for whatever reason, 'Moonlight Serenade' might happen to be played either on a record or over the radio, and the conversation would subside and a quiet would descend, and a pensive look would appear on the faces of those listening. It's very, very odd. Everyone present was a thousand miles away. Each adrift on his or her own private sea of memories, a panorama of bygone days rises irresistably to the surface, and I don't think there's a person in this whole wide world, if he's a bit gray around the temples, who doesn't feel a certain tug deep in his innermost being, listening to that song."*

After Glenn disappeared, his friend, Chummy MacGregor, quit playing and helped Helen Miller, who trusted him. Helen and Chummy eventually had an unfortunate falling out over issues concerning Glenn, which ruined their personal, but strictly platonic, relationship.

John Chalmers "Chummy" MacGregor, an important contributor to the great Glenn Miller Orchestra, passed on in 1973.

Mose Klink   Tex Beneke

Skippy Martin   Will Schwartz   Ernie Caceres

THE SAXOPHONE SECTION

	Instrument	Doubles	Played by
1.	B♭ Clarinet	E♭ Alto Saxophone	Will Schwartz
2.	E♭ Alto Saxophone	B♭ Clarinet	Skippy Martin
3.	E♭ Alto Saxophone	E♭ Baritone and B♭ Clarinet	Ernie Caceres
4.	B♭ Tenor Saxophone	B♭ Clarinet and B♭ Bass Clarinet	Mose Klink
5.	B♭ Tenor Saxophone	B♭ Clarinet	Tex Beneke

The Musicians
Ray Anthony

"I'll never forget that day in early 1941, getting the word that Glenn Miller would audition me. He always tried out likely prospects 'on the job,' and so I rushed downtown to New York's Hotel Pennsylvania, where the Miller band was playing the prestigious Cafe Rouge. In my excitement, I even hurtled the bandstand to get to the trumpet chair—causing a considerable loss of dignity all around."

Those are the words of Ray Anthony of Bentleyville, Pennsylvania, who came by his music naturally. We were standing in Jack Ellsworth's music library at radio station WLIM on Long Island in the mid 1980s. He said his dad first taught him to play at the age of five, starting on the trumpet. The Antonini family had their own orchestra composed of Ray's sister, two brothers, and their dad. Later on, Ray started and played in his own band when he was just fourteen. The other players

Richard Grudens and Ray Anthony at Radio WLIM - 1984

were in their twenties and thirties. Ray was strongly influenced by Louis Armstrong, and his out and out hero Harry James, whom he says was the "best damn trumpet player." But, Roy Eldridge stands alone as his teacher.

"I was way ahead of my time." said Ray. During high school, Ray played trumpet with local bands and quickly rose to the point where he was working as a featured trumpeter with Al Donohue's fine orchestra in Boston. At eighteen he joined the Jimmy Dorsey orchestra followed by his migration into the Glenn Miller organization.

"You had to play pretty good to land a job with Glenn Miller," I noted.

"I was a lot better than I even knew myself because...yes, you're right, Glenn Miller is not going to hire you because of your looks, or anything else except what you can do with your instrument. His was the number one band and I was with the Al Donohue band. I guess he had heard of me, so I thought I must be pretty good."

"Then why did you leave the band so quickly afterwards?"

"He fired me!"

"He *what*?" I was really surprised.

"With a thoughtful grin and a shake of the right shoulder: "He fired me."

"Why?"

"Well, that's hard to say. I don't think I was a bad guy, but I was obviously cocky...it might have been plain enthusiasm on my part, being so young and so excited to be there that I did things that didn't fall into line and I did other things like auditioning for Benny Goodman and Artie Shaw while I was with the band, just for the kick of doing it."

There was good reason for Ray's enthusiasm. To Ray Anthony the Glenn Miller band was the greatest in the business. His years with the Miller band was, for Ray, the best education anyone could have in playing popular music for a nation of young dancers.

Getting back to the story, the audition, for example, started with "Tuxedo Junction" which Anthony had heard but had never played. "I knew Glenn was a stickler for sight reading, and somehow, nervousness and all, I managed to get through it in acceptable style. Of course, I'll always remember that tune's infectious dancing mood, which the Billy May arrangement captures so well." Ray Anthony was always thrilled as the band played the first few bars of Glenn's beautiful theme, "Moonlight Serenade."

"Once at a radio show in Kansas City, the crowd reacted with a thrilling, riveting ovation when we played that theme. I had never heard anything like that before."

Glenn Miller rehired Ray Anthony a few months later in Cleveland because his influence in the brass section was strong. Miller had realized that Ray was a better musician than his replacement, Ralph Brewster. Glenn actually admired Ray Anthony's energy and enthusiasm. Ray remained a member of the band for a few years, only to be fired once again.

"He did it again," said Ray, laughing loudly, "Glenn was a disciplinarian whether it was in your playing, your mannerisms, or what you wore on the bandstand. He wanted and expected the best. He was much like {bandleader} Lawrence Welk, tight with a buck, although he paid me and his featured players enough, like Beneke, too, but other players weren't as happy. Glenn's great financial losses establishing his first band was probably the reason he was so frugal. He had lots of practice."

In the post World War II era, Ray Anthony formed a fast-rising dance band, despite the fact that the band business was in overall decline. His band followed the Glenn Miller mold like a number of other bands of the time and made good money touring the country's top spots. He went on to record with Capitol and built and promoted a good swinging band, featuring his own gutsy, low-register, Harry James style, horn.

Ray Anthony pioneered his craft by offering original music themes for some television shows in the 60s. His best-selling recordings of *Dragnet* and *Peter Gunn* are nothing short of sensational. During the period between 1950 and 1954, Ray had the number one band in the country.

In the mid-eighties Ray returned to touring: "The jobs are where they are and you have to go to them, that's always been true. That's where the people will be able to see you and get to know you. That's what Glenn Miller did and why his music is still valid today. And, it's great to play to different crowds."

Ray went into the mail order music business, something he called Big Band Eighties, that had over 2,500 listings, which has now changed. He's been a bandleader, a movie star, television performer, occasional stage actor, and entrepreneur. Ray is still active leading his band for private parties and occasional big band events. Bandleader Ben Grisafi always recommends Ray's band to California friends when they celebrate there and he can't make it. Ray directs the band himself.

Ray regularly hangs out with Hugh Hefner at the Playboy Mansion with friends Jerry Vale, Chuck McCann, Sid Caesar, Charles Durning, Harvey Korman, and Robert Culp, among others. They all seem to find comfort in the friendship of people they know for a long time. They watch old movies and entertain one another while having a great dinner.

Jerry Vale: "We have always been together over the years, enjoying each other's company. Over the years, we lost some of our friends, like Mel Tormé, but we move on as we must."

By the way, Jerry Vale has sung with the Glenn Miller Orchestra with Larry O'Brien, up at the Stardust Ballroom in the Bronx some years ago.

Ray Anthony has been a revelation in the music business and is still working his craft with enthusiasm.

"That's what keeps me young."

Jerry Vale and Richard Grudens - 2002
(photo R. Incagliato)

Reuben "Zeke" Zarchy
Trumpet

"So, I joined the Miller band as a trumpet player and I enjoyed it very much. I have to admit it was a little different than playing in Tommy Dorsey's band that I had come from. Tommy's band was probably the best band I ever worked in for balance, swing, you name it, and getting lessons every night from Tommy himself, whether we realized it or not."

Speaking to Reuben "Zeke" Zarchy this late July evening in 2003, from his home in Studio City, California, a place he said, "once I visited it after the war, I was determined that I would live here, even though I started my life in old New York."

Here's a true alumni of the original Glenn Miller Orchestra who had come up through the bands of Joe Haymes, Artie Shaw, Bob Crosby, Red Norvo, and Tommy Dorsey; then signed with Glenn, and later, played in Glenn's Army Air Force Band right through to the end when Glenn became lost forever.

"Glenn's was a static kind of band and, at the time, we were the most played, most recorded, becoming the most popular band in the country. In those days, a guy and his date would drive two hundred miles across the state of Iowa just to stand around and watch the band all night long. Glenn was the captain of the ship and he knew it would reflect on

Zeke Zarchy and Peanuts Hucko - 1945

us if we did not have our hair cut, or wear clean shirts, or have our suits pressed, so most of us kept ourselves pretty much in line."

Without any doubt, every musician had to look very good and play very well to remain employed in the Glenn Miller Orchestra. That's the way it was.

Zeke Zarchy has done it all as a stellar trumpet player. He has led the trumpet section in many of the bands in which he played. Bing's favorite bandleader, John Scott Trotter, selected Zeke to lead the trumpet section in his band that played on Bing Crosby's popular radio show.

When the movie "The Glenn Miller Story" was released, Zeke was disappointed, citing many inaccuracies of what he termed, "...a strictly made-up story of Glenn's life." The movie was a *Hollywood* version of Glenn's life and music with not much truth or fact. Zeke said it made more money for Universal Studios than any other film of the time. Many have said the movie probably saved Universal from financial disaster. Many musicians I have talked with that were involved with Glenn have refuted much of the movie's validity, especially with respect to the origination of the famous Miller *sound*, right up to the actual role of band pianist Chummy MacGregor, (played by Harry Morgan, later of M*A*S*H fame,) with respect to his relationship with Glenn. And, the introduction of clarinet player Willie Schwartz early in Glenn's career, auditioning for a spot in Ben Pollack's band years before Glenn established his band, was absolutely an impossibility with respect to his age. In fact, Willie joined Glenn's second band many years later.

Zeke Zarchy enjoyed a most respectable run as a top musician and was known as a reliable lead trumpeter of the Big Band Era. Beyond that time, Zeke Zarchy toured with the Miller reunion band, appearing at many engagements in Europe, Japan, and South America. During his tenure with the band, Zeke was a good and trusted friend to Glenn.

Al Klink

Saxophone

"I got into Glenn's band through Legh Knowles, a Miller trumpet player, who recommended me. We had worked together locally around Danbury, Connecticut. I had quit high school to go on the road with a band. I got started as trumpet player, but I was given up as hopeless by my teacher. He said I'd never make it, and to *forget it*. So I tried the next easiest instrument, the clarinet, and that's what I played."

Al Klink was generally left alone by Glenn, and Klink, reacting, acted likewise, like most of the band members. He always, nevertheless, tried his best to honor all Glenn's performance demands.

"You couldn't influence Glenn about anything. Some guys were close to him, but they were never on the same level. I know Chummy was a friend from their old days, but Glenn was generally aloof with most of us.

"Our sax section was probably one of the best that I ever sat in. Willie Schwartz and I, of course, were the two lead

"In the Mood" with Glenn, Klink and Beneke

voices. I played bottom tenor lead and Willie and I sat next to each other. We got to know the idiosyncrasies of each other's instruments. Willie knew the bad notes on my tenor and I knew the bad ones on his clarinet. We were sometimes too loud for the open brass, but we could blow pretty good. Glenn would remind us."

There were really no cliques in the band. The common enemy to some of the players was Glenn himself. These rebels felt united in some odd way. Chummy MacGregor abstained. Even Tex and Hal McIntyre joined with the rebels, although they stood in Glenn's favor. It was an unsaid standoff. But, Glenn always prevailed. His players were really young players that required big band business discipline.

"Drinking was well controlled. Glenn would get that way once a year or so. We really had no boozers, though. I would drink gin, because it looked like water disguised in the glass. The guys were really not paid well as some of the other bands. We made lots of money, however, because we were so busy. Over our salaries, we got extra fees for radio shows and recordings."

Glenn was always able to tell his musicians just what he wanted and required of his players. He was always on top of things. For him, it was a matter of balance with the inner voices of each section. It was very important for the players of inner voices to be meticulous about their parts. According to Klink: "It's a basic rule about any good section playing. It's a human tendency for guys not playing lead to slough it off. It just doesn't work because there's no such thing as an unimportant voice in a saxophone or brass section."

Rehearsals were reduced once everyone knew their part, and increased when new members were added. Glenn would never tell anyone how to play their solo's. He expected them to follow the chart, whether it was for eight or thirty-two bars.

"It's funny. I had the feeling that with Glenn we were like a corporation. He was the president and on a different floor than the rest of us.

"Because Glenn had a first bad experience with peer players, the band that finally made it was made up of mostly inexperienced kids that he could have his way with. We didn't know any better. He was the General and we were the troops.

"Glenn also had a lot of good attributes. He was kind to all. He was aware of the appearance of the band. He was intelligent. He understood showmanship. We had choreography, you know, waving the horns and all that. We didn't swing like Artie Shaw, and he understood that, too. All this worked for Glenn Miller."

Roland "Rolly" Bundock
Bass

The famous Miller sound wasn't there yet, but bass player Rolly Bundock was with the band when it was booked into the Blue Room of the Roosevelt Hotel in New Orleans. To give the band some local appeal, Miller had added jazz clarinetist Irving Fazzola to the band.

Rolly: "I was sitting in back of the regular saxophone section, and a lot of pretty things were written with the tenor lead on the bottom. One night, Miller asked Fazzola if he could play his part over his shoulder, that's the tenor lead part, and Fazzola says, 'Yeh!' So he told him to try playing along whenever he gets the lead, and to try playing along with him on clarinet, which would make it sound an octave higher. Well, Fazzola did that and I believe the so-called Miller sound had it's birth right there."

To put a band together is one thing, musically. Financially, it was another thing. Glenn needed financial help.

"The Shribman Brothers, Cy and Joe, did more for Glenn, I think, than any other group of people by backing his bookings. Miller wasn't making out too well. A practically unknown band doesn't acquire a following overnight and they couldn't get people behind them.

"At the Glen Island Casino and other places we did 364 one night stands in one year, something hard to believe. I think the major winning point for the band, insofar as success was concerned, was going into Frank Dailey's Meadowbrook in New Jersey, and from there into the Glen Island Casino. That made us. We were on the radio all over the country. And it made us big.

Rolly Bundock's take on Glenn was clear and simple: "He was the General MacArthur of the music business."

Legh Knowles

Trumpet

Sideman Legh, yes, LEGH, not misspelled, enjoyed playing the Glenn Miller ballads. He felt the band didn't really swing like Artie Shaw and Benny Goodman. "Glenn always had us playing so perfectly so we were never relaxed enough to really swing."

Legh joined up with Glenn for $ 75.00 a week. "Yeh, but when we were playing one night in Durham, North Carolina, playing at a dance, Glenn called me over and said, "'Who do you think you are? I'm paying real good musicians fifty bucks, and you're holding me up for seventy-five. You're going to get fifty dollars from now on.'

"You know, he intimidated me so much." Legh felt that Glenn was a very creative when he had the guts to construct a harmonization which became the *Glenn Miller sound*. With Bill Finegan and Jerry Gray, Legh said: "He gave them the pattern, and they wrote it, and the people loved it. It was enjoyable and memorable."

To Legh, the Glenn Miller Story was a Hollywood- style adventure, far from the truth and facts: "One of the scenes showed all the band flocking to his home in New Jersey. How stupid, in reality we didn't even know where he lived!

Glenn just dominated you. He was a real disciplinarian. He wouldn't talk to you, maybe for six weeks."

Legh Knowles also played with Charlie Spivak's Orchestra. In the mid-ninties, Legh was invloved with Beaulieu Vineyards in California. He has otherwise always been involved in the Big Band scene there.

Charlie Spivak
Trumpet

Charlie Spivak
(Hollywood photos)

Reflecting on Glenn's generosity, trumpeter Charlie Spivak speaks: "As far as my band was concerned, Glenn Miller is the man who was responsible for the whole thing. He was my guardian angel, he got the money for me so I could get started and had me booked into a place called the Glen Island Casino, the favorite spot for all the bands. It was my starting-off place. With Glenn's help, of course, I was fortunate enough to be able to go in there, which made it possible for me to make some kind of name for myself right off the bat."

Jimmy Priddy
Trombone

"At that time we usually played a new song quite a bit before we recorded it. On the job we had to rehearse and rehearse because Glenn knew we would be recording it.

The song pluggers were always pushing their tunes. If the tune was in Glenn's same style, it became a better reason why he would record or play it. So, he would try to get us to become familiar with a song because we would record it right after a show, that very same night. So we'd start at two o'clock in the morning. Always unbelievable."

Dale "Mickey" McMickle

Trumpet

About the recording session of April 18, 1939 "Stairway to the Stars" and "Pavanne."

"I am hard to get along with, so I had my differences with Glenn too, but, I had great respect for him, and as a result, we got along quite well. And, I enjoyed working for him. I enjoyed it very much, in fact, I think it was the highlight of my musical career. He wasn't a great trombone player but he was an excellent musician and a wonderful organizer. He knew how to get what he wanted from the fellows in the

Dale, Glenn and Willie Schwartz at CBS
(courtesy CBS)

band. Some of them resented it, and some of them didn't. I happened to be one who didn't—except on occasion.

"Playing with this band was kinda rough, but the band was a very popular band and had a lot of work. We'd be at the Pennsylvania Hotel three days a week, plus we'd do the Chesterfield radio program, then did shows at the Paramount and at the same time doing five shows a day. Actually, it was a little relaxing to get out on the road. We didn't have to work as hard. Of course, we had to travel. But, that was another story.

"Glenn didn't care about your drinking, as long as you did your work. I had been in the band for over three years as trumpet player. It was a very clean band and what you did on your own time, no matter, he didn't interfere. He never put down the law or told you not to drink or smoke stuff, but if you showed up late, God help you!"

Johnny Best
Trumpet

About the recording session of "Stardust" on January 29, 1940

"The first thing that I had anything that I could remember to play on was a solo on 'Stardust.' I had a half-a-chorus on that. I think the trumpet part was added on to the original arrangement. He had a one chorus arrangement on 'Stardust,' like for a medley, and he added the trumpet. I believe he changed keys on it. If I recall right, there is a tenor solo and an ensemble ending."

Johnny Best was a new addition to the trumpet section beginning on August 11, 1939, first playing during a recording session of "Melancholy Lullaby." Because the band was very popular, fans were always looking for autographs from band members after the show, but some players would ignore

THE BRASS SECTION

Four Trumpets	Four Trombones
R. D. McMickle	Frank D'Anolfo
John Best	Jimmy Priddy
Billy May	Paul Tanner
Steve Lipkins	Glenn Miller

them. Glenn didn't like that. He felt it would create ill feelings and felt they should honor autograph requests.

"So we did it, like it or not."

Wilbur "Willie" Schwartz

Sax, Clarinet

At twenty-one, Willie was the youngest musician in the Miller band.

"I had been working at the Roseland Ballroom in New York, and he came in one night and asked me if I'd like to join his band. He was just going to start out with the saxophone section and experiment and try to get that particular *sound* that he wanted so much. We started out with just the clarinet and the four saxophones and worked on that for about a week or two then he brought in the rest of the band.

"Then we rehearsed for about two or three more weeks and then left for Boston, and that's when we started one-nighters. Glenn showed us the ropes, he was experienced and we were just kids and we learned from him. We grew up with the band, none of us were married, none of us had children, we were just a bunch of kids on the road playing music with the best band in the land."

The clarinet work of Willie was becoming a trademark, part of the identifying *sound* of the band. "It wasn't just me, it was all five of us, four saxes and a clarinet. We all had to play together and breathe together and phrase together. There wasn't any feeling about being a soloist, or anything special. I was just one of the reeds. The whole idea was to try to make the five of us sound like one."

A young Willie Schwartz
(Movie Star News)

Willie Schwartz remains a legendary Glenn Miller musician.

Melvin "Mel" Powell
Piano

A tall, blonde hair, bespeckled Mel Powell, the piano player for the great Glenn Miller Army Air Force band, joined with Glenn after coming off playing and arranging with Benny Goodman's organization where he arranged some of Benny's great charts: "Mission to Moscow," "String of Pearls" and "Jersey Bounce."

Glenn, Ray McKinley and Mel Powell
(R. Grudens collection)

"Glenn's Air Force band was different than his civilian band. Ray McKinley's influence was a bit more jazz oriented than Glenn's. Glenn's band was beautiful, nice and interesting, but never jazzy. His was a dance band with exceptions. I think he liked having me in this new, great Air Force band because of my affiliation with Benny. I was a living link to one of his mentors."

Mel Powell was an extraordinary virtuoso pianist who later became a member of the faculty at the California Institute of Arts in Valencia, California, eventually becoming its Dean, as well as a respected composer of contemporary material.

"It was great playing with that band. We were all very young, mostly unmarried and without children. We had no responsibilities except to play the music we all loved. We had no other worries. And, we did crazy things. I remember once going up in a fighter plane with a friend. It had only one seat, so I sat on his lap. We chased some German fighters and flew just a few feet above the ground. We would fly with bomb bay doors open at 8,000 feet off the ground. Now, I look both ways when I cross the street.

"Despite hard times for us in England and hard work making records and performing for endless radio shows, the British people liked the band and its music. Today, there is a Glenn Miller band in England {1986}, that's how much they loved it. We had aspirations and felt excitement, unlike the young players of today. The world was different then, or maybe it was just us being so young and facing dangers with aplomb; I don't know."

Mel Powell was somewhat rebellious, resenting some of the strict regulations imposed by Glenn for all the musicians. Mel also led a small *inside the band group* called "Uptown Hall" featuring clarinetist and future bandleader, Peanuts Hucko, and trumpet player Bernie Privin, instituted by Glenn to vary the series of programs for the radio shows, something Mel enjoyed as a divergence from the regular playing in the entire concert orchestra.

My favorite Mel Powell album is his 1948 Capitol album #CC-37 *Mel Powell on Piano*. It provides a great variety of moods from the frantic "Way Down Yonder in New Orleans" to the quiet tones of "You Go to My Head." It's a worthwhile album, minus any vocals, if you can find it. Maybe on E-Bay? Somewhere.

Maurice "Moe" Purtill

Drums

Influenced by Jo Jones and Gene Krupa, Moe Purtill was a crucial player in the rhythm section.

"As far as I'm concerned, I believe that it was radio that made Glenn Miller—not the records, and not the movies. The records sold because folks heard us on the radio. Glenn's theory was: 'We go on the air as much as we can.' Sure, we made records, lots of them, but many more heard us on the radio from places like Glen Island and created the demand. Miller was not bothered much if the band was playing to houses that were half-empty, he was more concerned with the unseen radio audience who picked up their live, remote broadcasts right from where we were playing.

"Glenn would say, 'If they heard us, Moe, we're in, If we played your hometown, you'd think—That's the band we've been listening to every night.' You wanted to see what the hell you were listening to.

"We did twenty tunes at first. We kept pounding them into you. And then the people began calling out for tunes we'd never recorded. They knew them because they'd heard us play them on the broadcasts. And we'd record the numbers people would ask for."

Bobby Hackett
Cornet and Guitar

Bobby Hackett was probably the only jazz-orientated musician in Glenn's second band. This is what he told me:

"When I wanted to join his band, he didn't need any trumpet players. But, I eventually got me a gig. I was only playing guitar temporarily when I moved in with the brass.

I remember when we rehearsed for the recording of Jerry Gray's composition, 'String of Pearls.' I played cornet and broke the solo when I first ran it down." Bobby doesn't like to play a solo the same way twice, if he can help it. So, Glenn called him over and said, "Do you remember what you played on that?" "Well," Bobby said, "If I had to. Then, Glenn said, and I don't blame him for saying so, that it would be good if I played it that way all of the time. So, I usually played it that way just to please him."

Lloyd "Skip" Martin
Clarinet and Alto Sax

Indianapolis born Skip Martin came from Benny Goodman's band to become Glenn's new lead saxophone. A month before, he had been making records for the swinging Goodman band.

"The first thing I did with Glenn was a coast-to-coast broadcast 7:30 to 8:00 and I had to read from sight because I had never seen the book before. They had three different kinds of cuts. I didn't make a mistake, but I was just shocked."

Skip Martin was just getting adjusted to the band and played on the recording of "Keep 'Em Flying" on December 8, 1941, hours after Pearl Harbor was attacked. Although the lead alto man, Martin always felt like a newcomer, having worked in the band only the last ten months before it disbanded in September 1942.

"I never got to know Glenn very well. We weren't close at all. He was busy with his life and I was busy with mine. He had good musicians. I wasn't happy with him as I was with Benny."

Skip Martin settled in Los Angeles and got involved with studio work, contributing arrangements including the greatest Les Brown instrumental, "I've Got My Love to Keep Me Warm," in my opinion, one of the best recorded big band instrumentals of all time. Martin worked in movies and at NBC as a staff arranger. He conducted the sound track for the Fred Astaire film *Royal Wedding*, and produced material in albums for some of great jazz musicians on the West Coast. Skip Martin passed away in February of 1976 in Hollywood, California.

George Simon

Drums

Drummer, and sometimes member of the Glenn Miller Orchestra, played on Glenn's recording of "Sleepytime Gal," a 1937 Decca Recording. It was George Simon who would go on to write the definitive biography of his friend, Glenn Miller, in 1974. I spoke with him in 1999:

"I had just joined Metronome Magazine, and Glenn had just organized Ray Noble's band up at the Rainbow Room, sixty-five stories high up in Rockefeller Center, and I had to go back up there, into the back area where all the musicians rooms were quartered. Great musicians like Bud Freeman and Claude Thornhill, and Charlie Spivak and Will Bradley, and so forth. It was part of my job to get to know the various players in all the bands for material for my column in Metronome.

George Simon
(courtesy Metronome Magazine)

"Yes, I do remember, for some inexplicable reason, Glenn and I gravitated to each other and we became friends immediately. I was living at home with my family because I just got out of college and had just joined Metronome, and I would have musicians like Charlie Spivak up for dinner—and they were *real* folks. My folks were not at all jazz-oriented. They enjoyed classical music, but Glenn fit right in with them. They were crazy about him because he was a gentleman, and very much aware of things other than music.

"There was a place on Broadway and 49th Street, right in the heart of Times Square called the Paradise Restaurant, a kind of businessmen's restaurant. The Glenn Miller band in those days was hired to play there but was not the lead band. The featured band was not Glenn Miller, but Freddie Fisher's Spike Jones-like band, called the Schnickelfritzers. Although Glenn played for dancing and Fisher was the lead band, Glenn was able to get some airtime while there. His musicians would be so tired playing those lengthy shows, that by the time they got on the air, some of their lips were in pretty twisted condition."

We lost the voice of George Simon in 2002.

Glenn's Fine Arrangers
Bill Finegan, Jerry Gray and Billy May

According to Professor Richard Grudzinski of Berklee School of Music in Boston, Massachusetts: "Arranging is the art of adapting a musical composition to a specific instrumental and/or vocal combination. This may range from a single performer, a solo guitar or piano, to a full orchestra with a choir."

The American Heritage Dictionary defines arranger or arranging as: "Music. To reset (a composition) for other instruments or voices or for another style of performance."

Professor Grudzinski: *"Normally, the arranger works for a client, usually a singer."*

Besides Glenn Miller himself, three outstanding arrangers dominated the civilian band, Bill Finegan, Jerry Gray and Billy May.

Bill Finegan

As for Bill Finegan, he concludes the greatest thing that happened in his life was arranging music with Glenn Miller: "When I first joined him, I think, it was my attitude that made for a rough beginning, but, as we went along I got to know Glenn and he was very patient with me.

The heavy work load of the band at the time took a toll on the musicians and especially the arrangers. Add in the three times a week broadcasts for Chesterfield Cigarettes, which created an even heavier load on everybody.

Bill Finegan was a newcomer and first arranged Glenn's recording of "Romance Runs in the Family" on February 6, 1939, a date he will always remember, of course.

"Ironically, for me, that record was a dog. It was the first song I arranged for Glenn that was recorded, although I had done some radio shows earlier. I was always at the recording sessions when my arrangements were a part of it. Glenn would always want me there, sometimes just to make a few changes.

"I would sit in the booth with the mixer to try to get a good mix on the band. With the primitive equipment they had at that time, I used to say to Glenn, that if we had to depend on our records, we'd never make it because the recording sessions were usually disappointing. The band actually sounded better than it did on all those old recordings. But the people were nevertheless impressed. We must have been doing something right because the next month we were booked into Frank Dailey's Meadowbrook. That was an important event for us."

Bill Finegan also had a feeling for "Little Brown Jug," in that the recording would make it big. "But, I don't remember how we got a hold of that tune and decided to record it, but I remember 'Sunrise Serenade,' which I also arranged."

The tune, of course, was an old ditty written in 1869 by Joseph Winner. "Sunrise Serenade" was harmonically a very simple song. It could be harmonized in intervals of a third, which, for most people is a very easy interval to hear, but probably that was one of the things that made "Sunrise Serenade" successful. Bill Finegan hated to analyze his successes or failures after the fact. He could almost always predict the outcome of some of his arrangements.

Bill was the only arranger working for Glenn when "Stairway to the Stars" was recorded on May 9, 1939. He had so much to do at the time when the orchestra was cranking out all those RCA Bluebird recordings. He worked mostly at night when it was quiet, and like others, sometimes all night long. He usually arranged with a piano, but sometimes without it if they were in a hotel room where there was none. That's how good he was at his craft, running the music through his head as an architect does with his own schemes and dreams. Bill's "Volga Boatman," "Pavanne," "Skylark," and "Runnin' Wild," and with Jerry Gray, "Serenade in Blue," (with help on the introduction by Billy May,) arrangements enjoyed long runs and became Glenn Miller standards that are part of the permanent book and played at performances regularly. With Bill Finegan, Glenn arranged Hoagy Carmichael's all-time evergreen tune, "Stardust." Bill Finegan had clearly arranged some great works for the Glenn Miller orchestra and has earned his place among the great musicians who made up the Glenn Miller Orchestra.

To assist an overworked Bill Finegan, Glenn obtained the talents of Jerry Gray from the Artie Shaw band which had just broken up.

Jerry Gray

Jerry Gray—*who introduced radio's most popular big band novelty feature—"Something Old, Something New, Something Borrowed, Something Blue," a specialty heard regularly on Glenn's radio broadcasts.*

Jerry Gray, fresh from Artie Shaw's band, had already earned his arranging stripes working out the Artie Shaw blockbuster hit "Begin the Beguine" one of the most popular recordings of the era.

"I heard about the Miller Band when they were playing at the Meadowbrook, and he called me up and offered me a job—so I went out there and caught the band. The Miller Band didn't sound like my favorite band, which was Shaw. So I kept stalling him for a couple of weeks, but finally I decided to join him because I needed the money. So Glenn immediately assigned me to do most of the arrangements. There were a lot of ballads and stuff, 'Elmer's Tune' and 'Something Old, Something New, Something Borrowed, Something Blue,' that became a staple on the radio show. Those were mostly my medleys. I didn't like doing it at first, because I figured he was throwing crumbs at me, but, later, I realized my services were more valuable than I first thought."

Of course, Glenn himself had arranged some of the band's hits, "Moonlight Serenade," "Bugle Call Rag," and "King Porter Stomp." With pianist Chummy MacGregor, Glenn co-arranged the band's excellent version of "Danny Boy," on which he solos beautifully. Jerry Gray arranged some very important songs for the band. Jerry's own composition, "String of Pearls," and "Chattanooga Choo Choo," "Don't Sit Under the Apple Tree," "Pennsylvania 6-5000," "Tuxedo Junction," "My Isle of Golden Dreams," "Little Brown Jug," "Kalamazoo," and "Runnin' Wild," were just the big ones. "Beautiful Ohio" was the first Miller record arranged by Jerry Gray.

"Glenn did very little editing with me, Artie Shaw did more of it. After a while he left me more or less on my own. He allowed me sort of a free hand. But of course when we rehearsed them, he put some final touches on it." Jerry Gray wound up arranging in the Army Air Force Band with Major Glenn Miller.

Jerry: "I wrote 'String of Pearls' when I was young and still single, living at home near Boston. My parents were

Fans remember the pleasing sound of "String of Pearls" as an unmistakable Miller sound with the light but strong beat and that special trumpet solo of Bobby Hackett. The super introduction moves an octave lower each opening beat and sets up the melody, played in harmony with three saxophones.

at the movies and I sat down at the piano in the dark and it came to me, the whole thing—introduction, melody, and arrangement. By the time my folks came home I had the whole thing in my head. It was that simple, just took me a couple of hours. Then Glenn got it and changed it a little bit here and there and we added Bobby Hackett's trumpet which really helped a lot. The thing became an instant success so Glenn put me on composing instead of just arranging. 'A String of Pearls,' I guess, was the fastest work I ever did—the fastest and biggest."

Billy May

"For me, the money was good and the band was good, so I signed on and stayed for two years, but I enjoyed playing with the Charlie Barnet band more than I enjoyed my time with Glenn Miller."

On the 8th of November, 1940, Billy May signed with the Glenn Miller band. It was election eve and business wasn't expected to be very good that evening.

In Glenn's band, Billy May essentially played trumpet, of course, but also shared arranging chores with Bill Finegan and Jerry Gray.

"Glenn would usually assign songs he needed to the regular arrangers, Bill Finegan and Jerry Gray, because that was their job. He kept telling me to 'write an original...write an original.'"

As a result, Billy literally altered the band musically with different and innovative arranging material. "The band was playing kind of stiff, but I changed that a bit."

Billy May's enthusiasm and loose arrangements were more inventive, carefree and jazzy. He interjected a lilting, swinging quality in his arrangements that the musicians relished. His first arrangement with Glenn was a swinging rendition of "Ida" with Tex Beneke on the vocal that is now considered a Miller *standard.*

In discussing the subject of arranging with Billy May a few years ago, he described the job of arranging to me:

"When someone like Irving Berlin writes a song, they usually write just the piano part. If a vocalist is added, they can simply work it out. But, an arranger takes that song and does the background of, say, an instrumental version, keeping in mind perhaps the addition of a vocalist—figures the key and the vocalists range, and, depending on the mix of instruments you employ, arranges it accordingly."

Willie Schwartz

"One of the biggest steps to success was when Billy May joined the band from Charlie Barnet. Glenn allowed him to write some arrangements and he brought in a whole new concept of playing. We were just slogging along with ballads and trying to play swing music and weren't quite making it. Billy was a fresh, young arranger who inspired the band. We, and Glenn, were glad to find him."

Billy: "We made an awful lot of records when I was with Glenn. I made arrangements of all the stuff from the two pictures, *Sun Valley Serenade* and *Orchestra Wives.*

Margaret Whiting, Billy May and Friend

We recorded all the pre-scoring and the post scoring at 20th Century Fox and then went out to Sycamore and waxed all the 'Chattanooga Choo Choo' material. 'Chattanooga Choo Choo' and 'Kalamazoo' were both big, long production numbers. I remember seeing the pictures and the Nicholas brothers dancing, and we played all that in the picture and the Miller Band actually performed it. I worked on some of those things with fellow arrangers Jerry and Bill. It was so long that we each took a hunk to work on. The choreographer laid it out and we went to work." But, Glenn cut some of them down to make them more commercially acceptable.

(courtesy Capitol Records)

"Glenn chose the best parts, of course, which was usually the front part and the ending. So we made all those very well. Paula Kelly was in the band as a Modernaire then, although Marion Hutton was the featured vocalist. I think Marion dropped out to have a baby or something. Paula sang some of the vocals there. She was a marvelous singer, as good a singer as anyone around, and I remember she did a couple of the solos, and I was happy she was getting a chance to do some solo work with the band. This recording was arranged by Jerry Gray and Bill Finegan."

Paula Kelly

"We had come out to California and I had to join the band enroute, as a matter of fact, in St. Louis. The band was making their first movie, *Sun Valley Serenade*. It was very exciting and thrilling to me. And I was real pleased that Glenn had enough confidence in me to let me sing 'I Know Why.' It was a beautiful song and I was very flattered by the whole thing."

Paula had momentarily replaced Dorothy Claire, and was a temporary replacement for Marion Hutton.

I KNOW WHY (AND SO DO YOU)
Mack Gordon & Harry Warren

You possess a magic something
That has me spellbound when you are near
Just a certain charming something
When you're beside me miracles appear
For when I look at you,
Life's a grand illusion
(refrain)
Why do Robins sing in December
Long before the Springtime is due?
And even though it's snowing
Violets are growing
I know why and so do you
Why do breezes sigh every evening
Whispering your name as they do?
And why have I the feeling
Stars are on my ceiling?
I know why and so do you.
When you smile at me
I hear gypsy violins
When you dance with me
I'm in heaven when the music begins
I can see the sun when it's raining
Hiding every cloud from my view
And why do I see rainbows when you're in my arms?
I know why and so do you.

Paula Kelly fared well with Glenn on the recordings "Sweeter Than the Sweetest" in 1941 with the Modernaires, and with "The Booglie Wooglie Piggy," also with the original fab four, and on "Delilah," and "It Happened in Sun Valley," once again with the Mods.

Billy would place a pseudonym on many of his Miller arrangements, because of a contractual condition with his first wife, Arletta. Rather than implementing an entirely fictitious name, he often employed the name of Arletta May, in order to keep the *May* name on the recording, listed as arranger. And that's exactly how they are listed in the Miller catalog.

In Hollywood, CA, 1941 Making *Sun Valley Serenade*. The band with Paula Kelly. *(courtesy 20th Century Fox)*

Ironically, he awarded the tunes he arranged to Arletta as part of his divorce settlement, and when the Glenn Miller Story movie was made, it was Arletta alone who cashed in on her former husband Billy's tunes. He received nothing at all.

And, let's not forget Billy's exceptional introduction written for Glenn's "Serenade in Blue" recording. It is my favorite, specially crafted song introduction.

"I put it together in about fifteen min-

Paula Kelly with the Mods *(R. Grudens collection)*

utes during one rehearsal, after Glenn had assigned it to all three of us. He tried mine first and liked it, not that it was really any better than the ones written by Jerry (Gray) or Bill (Finegan).

> *Later, in Chicago, when the band arrived in the mid-summer and recorded six sides at the RCA Victor studio, they were also working at the College Inn at night. Sometimes they all had to get up at nine o'clock after working until two the night before.*

"It was really rough. But we got a lot of really good records in there. Billy Finegan wrote some really good arrangements. But things were coming to an end. Even Ray Eberle decided to leave there and then. And there was talk about a recording strike." Yes, they recorded some great arrangements in that final period: "That Old Black Magic," and on July 16th 1942, the last recording date, "I'm Old Fashioned," "A Pink Cocktail for a Blue Lady," "Rainbow Rhapsody," "Sleepytown Train," and Bill Finegan's version of "Rhapsody In Blue," that includes a great clarinet solo by Bobby Hackett, who

Billy May and his Orchestra
(R. Grudens collection)

refused to take credit for Bill Finegan's efforts. Otherwise, it was the very last commercial record made by the Glenn Miller civilian band.

For Billy May, a singer like Frank Sinatra, besides being a very good singer, is really a better musician—with fine musical taste, more than people gave him credit for. He would sit with an arranger, like May, whom he admired, for hours and work out what he wants the song to sound like. Does he want to do a ballad with strings, or does he want to work with a dance band sound?

Billy May remains one of the most prolific arrangers of the age. He has worked with Nat "King" Cole, who recorded over 60 to 70 sides on the *Billy May Sessions* albums, and on Peggy Lee's album *Pretty Eyes*, as well as Frankie Laine's work at Columbia, and on Billy Eckstine's *Roulette Album*, Vic Damone's *Strange Enchantment* album, Ella Fitzgerald's various albums, and, of course, many fine Frank Sinatra recordings. Billy May's arrangements of Sinatra albums are considered some of the singer's best works, including the albums "Sinatra Swings" and "Come Swing with Me." All these vocalists owe a great deal to Billy's arranging skills.

> *"With all those singers and bands, it's always a meeting of the minds. You work together to produce the sounds you both want to achieve."*

Billy began very young in music playing a tuba in high school, but wound up blowing a trumpet: "I became intrigued with the makeup of orchestrations and began making arrangements by the time I was fourteen. I could always tell what the music would sound like in my head. I would utilize the band instruments available in a given band to reach the best effect.

Billy May began arranging for Ozzie Nelson's early radio show. He wrote arrangements for the powerhouse Charlie Barnet band, setting the band's style, and for John Scott Trotter's orchestra on Bing Crosby's famous radio show, including his work with Bing on some Decca recordings.

Efforts to operate and lead his own band in 1951 were disappointing, as the big band era was literally winding down. When lucrative Hollywood work became available, he rushed to become a studio musician and arranger.

"I've been here in Hollywood ever since." He talked about it to me one cool November day from his home in San Clemente, California:

"When I first worked in Hollywood, I would arrange works around the ability of the excellent players who were employed in the established studio bands, so it became easy to get them to accomplish what was needed for a given project."

Sure, Billy May preferred arranging for the more jazzier bands, but his contributions to the original Miller charts are legendary and have outlasted in popularity over all other work's he performed since. Those charts have held up over all others and are played every day somewhere in the world by one of the Glenn Miller Orchestras.

We lost Billy May in late January 2004. He remains one of the Big Band Era's most influential musical arrangers. Although he gained fame for his Charlie Barnet wailing and scooping saxophones voiced in thirds, and for his version of Ray Noble's "Cherokee," that became a standard in jazz circles, his stellar trumpet playing on Glenn's "American Patrol," and his written intro to Glenn's "Serenade in Blue" is more than enough proof to me that his playing and arranging days in the Glenn Miller Orchestra of 1940-1942 helped elevate the stature of the band during it's most prolific and successful days.

THE VOCALISTS
Marion Hutton

Marion Hutton, sister of film performer Betty Hutton, was Glenn's prime singer. Glenn first introduced Marion as *Sissy Jones*, but backed off realizing it was too corny a name. Marion was just seventeen, so Glenn and Helen became Marion's legal guardian in order to allow her to tour with the band. Marion was also dubbed "...the sweetheart of the band," and had the nicknames of *Goldilocks*, the *Brat*, *The Whack*, *Tootsie-Roll*, *Rosebud*, *Snow White*, and even the *Dopey Duchess*, some mean and some keen, but all silly. She was totally revered by everyone as one of the nicest girl singers in the business.

Glenn, Marion and the Mods
(R. Grudens collection)

Moe Purtill: "Everybody respected Marion and teased her. Sometimes on the bus there would be some strong language spoken, but she'd sit right there up front and not say a thing. She was a gem."

Glenn had great confidence in Marion and featured her as an all-American girl and worried little about her singing skills. Marion felt that she was more an entertainer than premier vocalist, especially since Glenn featured her on all the corny Miller charts. Once, when Marion sought help from a vocal coach, Glenn noticed she was singing differently and admonished her, demanding she return to the regular way she sang. Marion felt she was literally owned by Glenn.

"As a singer, I provided something that distracted the public from the over-preciseness of the band. That was really why Glenn had me. It wasn't so much for my singing, although the thrust was to have pretty vocals. He liked Ray very much, too. I was young, pretty, vivacious, and full of energy and life, and I had a good time. I did a lot of things on the bandstands, like dancing, and so on-that the fans enjoyed."

Glenn worked her and the band very hard, which was one of the principle reasons for the band's success. "Glenn was a taskmaster and a perfectionist. He would never stand for anything but your best performance. He demanded that of himself, and he expected perfection from everyone, every time. Like a loving father, he taught me discipline, too. If you were sitting on the bandstand, you could see he was very disciplined, himself. There was another Glenn underneath that he didn't show to the outside world."

But, because of this disciplined hard work everyone became exhausted. From working the massive New York Paramount through their great moments in Carnegie Hall, so much hostility dominated the band personnel because everyone was simply worn out; emotionally, mentally, and physically. Marion would make a few comments before they went on, saying, "What a miracle this would be if we made it through this or that performance."

Despite the fact that Glenn loved Marion and her performances. Marion was not always a contented member of the band: "When it came to making recordings, I must confess—I never recorded anything I ever really liked. But, I wish Glenn was around now (1983) because he was so intense about the performances of his band, the business with the band, and his school teacher, serious side, that he could never let himself show his feelings to be seen by anyone. In the long run, I found him to be a beautiful, soft, warm, human being, something that very few people knew or understood about Glenn Miller."

Marion Hutton later discovered she was a terrific group vocalist. When Chuck Goldstein left the Modernaires, Glenn insisted Marion sing with the group, saying they looked better with her presence while on stage, so she sang all the leads that Goldstein used to sing.

"They say that I sparked the group. I enjoyed singing with the Mods, and found that I was really good at doing this, especially on the tune 'The Old Assembly Line' and 'Don't Sit Under the Apple Tree' that we recorded back in 1942.

"We were good. We never worried how it was going to turn out. It was difficult to know if you were going to have a hit or not. You'd think it's good, and you record it, then hope the public will feel the same way. We knew, for instance, that 'Lamplighters Serenade' was going to be very good, and it was. It was a perfect song for me and the Modernaires."

The song "That's Sabotage" was supposed to be featured in the movie *Orchestra Wives* being written expressly for Marion Hutton. It was arranged as a big musical number, but the War Department, or someone who managed the censoring of such things during the war, decided it was detrimental, not that it would've been. They were very careful about the proliferation of some such material, so Marion lost her big moment.

Dorothy Claire

Dorothy Claire's most impressive musical statement, vocalizing the beautiful Jerry Gray arrangement "Perfidia," recorded with the Modernaires, was written by Alberto Dominguez. Dorothy had joined the band after Marion

Hutton discovered she was pregnant and announced her retirement.

Dorothy was a pert blond with an outgoing personality. They say that she did not hit it off personally with Glenn, perhaps because Glenn and the band sorely missed Marion. Nevertheless, Dorothy Claire was a quality singer and expressed her positive personality while she was with Glenn. Dorothy was the object of a lawsuit against Glenn by bandleader Bobby Byrne from whom he allegedly stole Dorothy away. Glenn finally relented and Dorothy returned to the Bobby Byrne band.

She was replaced by Hal Dickenson's pretty wife, Paula Kelly. Paula joined the band in St.Louis, just before filming *Sun Valley Serenade*. Her rendition of "I Know Why-And So Do You" from that film remains a Miller classic and assures her a place in Glenn Miller's music history.

Kathleen Lane recorded with Glenn's early band "Every day's a Holiday," "Doin the Jive," and "Sweet Stranger" in 1937.

Gail Reese, Virginia Vonne, and statuesque Linda Keene were short-lived, but effective vocalists with Glenn Miller.

Ray Eberle

At the age of seventeen, and before completing high school, Ray Eberle found unexpected employment in the Glenn Miller Orchestra as its traditional boy vocalist. His brother, Bob Eberle, was already singing on top recordings with Jimmy Dorsey after the Dorsey's split to go on their own. The Eberle's, or Eberly's, were born in upstate New York. When Bob turned professional, he employed the name of *Eberly*. When Ray became a singer with Miller, he decided to use *Eberle, the original family name*, to distinguish him from his then famous brother.

Ray had gone to New York City for the first time when brother Bob called him to come visit him for a few days while

Ray, Glenn, Marion and Tex recording
(R. Grudens collection)

the Jimmy Dorsey band, with Bob as vocalist, was engaged at the Hotel New Yorker singing evergreens "Amapola," and "Maria Elena," "Green Eyes" with his singing partner Helen O'Connell.

"I was thrilled. The room was dimly lit and Bob was on the bandstand. I came into the room and walked past where Glenn Miller was sitting and talking to Jimmy Dorsey's manager. Glenn noticed me and did a double take, saying: "I know Bob Eberly is singing up there, but I swear he just walked past me."

Jimmy's manager explained that it was Bob's brother, Ray. Glenn promptly inquired: "Does he sing, too?"

"Glenn was no big deal bandleader then. When he learned I also sang, he asked me to come up to a rehearsal at the Haven Studio, and inquired if I would be interested in singing with his newly formed band. I sang a couple of tunes and he offered me a job paying $35.00 a week. It seemed like a lot of money to me at the time. I told him I would have to ask my father. I did and my father told me, 'It's your life and that's pretty good money.' The rest, as they say, is history."

Ray Eberle's first recording with Glenn was "Don't Wake Up my Heart" at the Haven Studio in New York.

> *The old Haven Studio was a combination recording studio and waiting room with old stuffed chairs and quirky furniture, decorated like a Chinese restaurant in old Hong Kong. The studio was like an old and large empty barrel. The one sure thing in the studio of any value was an old, but well-tuned piano and a couple of old chairs. Haven was located on West Fifty-fourth Street. Glenn had regularly rehearsed there. You had to walk up one flight where it was dingy and always dark, but it was very familiar territory for the boys in the band.*

Although Bob and Ray both participated in school plays on holidays, neither had ever taken vocal lessons. To Ray, Glenn was a fatherly figure who called him "Jim" for some unclear reason, and regularly introduced him as "The young man in the romance department."

"Glenn would say things to me like 'Jim, your ears are peaking,' which meant I needed a haircut. And he would say, during a set, 'Hey, kid, sing the words like they're written.' He was really good to me. When the success of 'In the Mood' caught fire, I got an immediate raise from $35.00 to $50.00, which was incredible at the time. It kept going up from there. We would do up to three record dates a day, starting early in the morning."

Ray Eberle was compensated very little for recording dates, being paid $15.00 per side, two for $25.00. He recorded something like 300 sides. Ray's favorite recordings were those selections from the

Glenn and Ray Eberle
(R. Grudens collection)

film *Orchestra Wives*: "Serenade in Blue," "At Last," "A Nightingale Sang in Berkeley Square" and "Everything I Love," songs, he said, "that I could sink my teeth into, and make a story out of so you could go to a crescendo and really make something out of it."

The pitch on some songs was too high for Ray's voice, but Glenn demanded exactness, with Ray taking no liberties, otherwise he would get tangled up with things going on behind him. Ray thought that Glenn moved the tempos along too fast for the ballads he had to sing, but Glenn was clearly in charge. Ray started out with a high voice but, after some experience, gradually brought his voice down when needed.

Ray's account of why he left the band in 1942, just before Glenn closed shop and joined the Army Air Force, was explained in a much later interview:

"I left because of money differences, in that Glenn would not pay me for a movie even though I was under contract that stated that I was to be paid whether I worked or not. My fifteen year contract stated that when the band broke up he would retain 25% of me for the remainder of the contract. I brought my contract to the union after I quit in Chicago, explaining what had happened and they tore it up saying that Glenn owed me $5,000.00, but I was happy to be out of the contract. I didn't care, and my relationship with Glenn continued with no animosity. That proves how good our relationship was in the first place."

At one moment in time Ray thought he possessed a unique singing voice destined to put all other vocalists out of business. Just before they went on the air at the Paradise, Glenn explained that after they recorded the tunes performed on the radio show, they would be played back in the hotel suite to see how everyone did.

"I had two or three tunes on the air and I came on, and at the same time, Bing Crosby had a picture where he sang 'On the Sentimental Side.' So, I was going to thrill everybody in the audience and in the orchestra. I went up to Glenn's suite afterwards, where we all sat around on the couch and bed and whatnot, and the playback came on. And I'll tell you something, if I had been able to crawl out of that place underneath the door, I'd have done it."

With all due credit, Ray was a fine singer, especially on tunes like "Moonlight Cocktail," "Serenade in Blue," and "Skylark," all definitive versions of each song, Ray enjoying his best range and feeling.

Ray Eberle's last recording with the Miller band was "Yesterday's Gardenias," recorded on June 17, 1942, only a few months before the band disbanded due to Glenn losing musicians to the draft, an impending musicians recording strike, and Glenn volunteering for the Army Air Force where he would try and build a big band. The members of Glenn Miller's great orchestra were almost relieved.

A footnote: Bob and Ray had another singing brother, Walter, who sang, but never with any big name band.

Kay Starr

Singing and Recording Early on for the Glenn Miller Orchestra

"Mom and I went into the lobby of the Plymouth Hotel where we met Glenn Miller and agreed to sing with the band. I was only sixteen years old. I sang with the band for ten days. I was too dumb and too young and I didn't realize that the song 'Baby Me,' arranged by Bill Finegan, was too high-pitched for me. It was a tone and a half higher than I could handle, which was really Marion's range. I don't know where I got those notes from."

It was back in the late 1980's when I first met up with Kay Starr, the "Wheel of Fortune" gal, who was a one time vocalist with Glenn Miller. We talked about that recording date. Apparently Marion Hutton was ill, and had collapsed on the bandstand from nervous indigestion while the band was playing at the Glen Island Casino.

Cordially
Kay Starr

However, a record date had to be kept, so sixteen year old Kay Starr kept the date. You might have a hard time realizing it was Kay on both sides of that recording of "Baby Me" and "Love With a Capital You" because it was a pre-Charlie Barnet Kay Starr who would change her voice forever, after over-working her pipes on those harsh and mighty arrangements performed with Barnet's band.

"After singing for three years with Charlie, and you're singing over George Siravo's arrangements, you can bet that it affected my throat. It actually ruined my voice temporarily...a lot of people said that it made me sound different...the keys didn't change, so...I don't know." For Kay, ignorance was bliss. Charlie would tell her, "So your throat's bad...so what..sing anyway," And she unfortunately listened to him and had to have her voice retrained after developing polyps, which formed a throaty sound, which, ironically is really her trademark and unmistakably defines her.

"Or," she said, "maybe I just grew up. I had to take a year to recover, starting with piano and then added a bass, then drums, with no sticks, then just brushes for more weeks before I was able to sing with a

Richard Grudens interviews Kay Starr - 1985

full-blown orchestra. It was like learning to walk from a crawl."

The Glenn Miller recordings had Kay sounding lighter and brighter, but too high in range, unlike her later vocal persona. She never sounded that way again on any commercial recording.

As for her relationship with Glenn: "Glenn Miller didn't talk very much. At the time he was the biggest band in the world. He didn't talk to the guys in the band much, either, and seemed to be a solemn man. He was a leader, so it was a fact that there were no *buddies* in the band. You were there, you did your job, you kept your nose clean, your shoes shined. Nobody ever missed a beat."

Aside from "Wheel of Fortune," Kay Starr did very well on her recordings of "Side-By-Side," "Bonaparte's Retreat," and "The Rock and Roll Waltz."

"Every time I start to sing those tunes, somebody reaches over and touches somebody next to them, or they just smile, and you can just feel the memories starting, you know, and you can't deny that's what it's all about."

"A singer is no more than an actor set to music, because you are only as good as the story you tell, and people like to hear things they can identify with, and that's the story.

Kay is now a long way from her only Glenn Miller memory, but remembers it well. Speaking to her recently from her long time and snug Los Angeles home, she says she won her fame after that and is still going strong, continuing telling her stories to music.

Patty, Maxine and LaVerne

The Andrews Sisters - Patty, Maxene and LaVerne.
(R. Grudens collection)

The Andrews Sisters

The Andrews Sisters

In 1939, when Glenn Miller first began broadcasting the Chesterfield radio show, *Moonlight Serenade*, on Tuesday, Wednesday and Thursday evenings, the Andrews Sisters, Patty, Maxene and LaVerne were the featured singers. Chesterfield was concerned that Glenn's orchestra alone could not sustain the show without a name guest. As a result, the show was a great success. Patty said the girls received a huge amount of fan mail during the series. The shows originated from the CBS Playhouse radio studio on Broadway and Fifty-third Street in New York. It was not, however, the first time the girls had performed with Glenn. They had earlier toured briefly with him traveling to cities in the Northeast on one night stands. Twelve minutes of the fifteen minute show was allotted to Glenn and cigarette commercials, and three minutes went to the girls spot. Glenn wanted the script to be minimized and the music maximized.

Patty told me that Glenn and the girls got along nicely although he was not fond of their particular singing style. According to Larry Bruff of the advertising agency who handled Chesterfield Cigarettes, the Andrews Sisters were constantly bickering with one another, and as a result they were dropped from the show after thirty-eight performances. The agency was convinced, by that time, that Glenn and his orchestra could carry the show alone. The quabbles usually centered around things like how a song should end, or which scat arrangement should be used on this or that tune and, how to best compliment a song. As Patty once said, "We argued and fought just like any other sisters."

It wasn't very long after, as a result of the great public response to the Chesterfield shows, the girls were booked into the New York Paramount Theater with the Glenn Miller Orchestra. The shows were performed in the same format as the radio show, and were always sold out. For the paying public it was Glenn Miller and his Orchestra with the superstar Andrews Sisters—how could it fail?

Patty: "All of us loved Glenn. He was a tough customer, very disciplined. When he was lost over the English Channel, we sent our sympathy to his wife, Helen. We thought of Glenn Miller as a friend."

Glenn with the Andrews Sisters
(courtesy RCA Victor)

Maxene: "Glenn's demand for perfection reflected itself when he wanted to head to Paris to set the band up for GI performances. Another, less demanding conductor might not have cared to go ahead, so Glenn might still be with us today, who knows."

I, however, have always been in love with the Andrews Sisters. Ever since I first heard Patty, Maxene and LaVerne vocalize "Bei Mir Bist Du Schon," it was the beginning of my long running affection for them. The song means that you're grand. The three gals from Minneapolis belonged to me from that day forward. Their recordings punctuated my life at many meaningful milestones. For millions of others during World War II they were the definitive female strains of the era, the way Glenn Miller was as a big band.

They sang with Bing, they sang with Glenn, they sang alone. Remember "Rumors Are Flying," "Rum and Coca-Cola," "Beer Barrel Polka," "Hold Tight," the definitive "I'll Be With You in Apple Blossom Time," "Boogie Woogie Bugle Boy," "Ferryboat Serenade?" And how about their recordings with Bing, beginning with "Ciribiribin," then "Pistol Packin' Momma," "Don't Fence Me In," "Apalachicola, FLA," and "South America, Take It Away." There were more.

Jack Kapp, who ran Decca Records, had the girls record regularly and with many other artists, like Bing, that made them the most prolific artists of the era. The girls also recorded with the top bands of Benny Goodman, Tommy Dorsey, and Woody Herman.

Over the years, Patty Andrews and I have been pretty close. In 1985, my first magazine article about the girls as a result of my long interview with Patty, became their sales tool when seeking new bookings. Today, Patty lives in California with her piano player manager and devoted husband, Wally Weschler. They frequently attend local big band reunions.

Patty: "We, Bing Crosby, and the Glenn Miller Orchestra were such a part of everybody's life in the second World War. We represented the voice of home overseas and at home, we represented the spirit of the times in a musical way—a sort of security."

Patty is the only remaining Andrews sister. We lost LaVerne in 1967 and Maxene in 1995.

Today's Patty Andrews with husband Wally Weschler
(R. Grudens collection)

Bing Crosby and Glenn Miller

On August 31, 1944, three and a half months before Major Glenn Miller disappeared while on a single engine plane flying across the English Channel on his way to Paris to set things up for the band's forthcoming trip to perform for the troops, Bing Crosby met up with him and Sergeant Jerry Gray, the band's arranger, in England. Old friends, Bing felt honored when Glenn asked him to perform a few numbers with the American Band of the Allied Expeditionery Force Orchestra on *The Moonlight Serenaders* radio broadcast emanating live from a BBC radio studio. For many years the whereabouts of the 16" transcription disc of this broadcast was thought lost or destroyed. During the war, because of metals shortages, the "V" discs were not usually preserved. Instead, they were generally scrapped after being broadcast to the troops so the metal discs could be re-coated and thus re-used for subsequent broadcasts.

Glenn and Bing had been fellow performers back in the 1930s when Bing was a band vocalist and Glenn sat in the brass section, and serving sometimes as band arranger. They recorded some sides together for Brunswick Records, with Bing, of course, on the vocal, and Glenn, a well sought after studio musician, on slide trombone.

Bing was impressed with the quality musicianship of the Army Air Force band, something you could count on when Glenn Miller was directing.

Mark Scrimger of Club Crosby wrote the liner notes for the *album* "Bing Crosby with Glenn Miller and the American Band of the Allied Expeditionery Force Orchestra," when it was issued after the disc was recovered.

"Not unlike finding a pot of gold, the release of this 'lost broadcast' is a treasure designed to gladden the hearts of the legions of Bing Crosby and Glenn Miller enthusiasts all over the world," Mark wrote, "It is believed that this single broadcast recording was the only one on which Bing and Miller performed together as established stars."

> **Glenn: (Speaking on the air):** *"Here we are on another of your very own shows on your very own radio network, and over in the corner of the studio, outfitted in gas mask, tin hat, bed roll and B-4 bag is Bing Crosby, which all means that Bing is on his way to pay you fighting men a personal visit. But, we managed to snag him before we take off. Nothing I could say would top what feelings you have expressed about this guy, so I will just lay it on the line, short and sweet: Here's Bing Crosby."*

Bing, followed by an illustrious introduction from Major Miller himself, swung into "Long Ago and Far Away," arranged by Generoso Graziano, aka Jerry Gray. Bing slipped even deeper into the Miller mood with a part in one of the famous Miller medley's, "Something old, Something new, Something borrowed, Something blue," which included Something old: Gus Kahn and Walter Donaldson's "My Buddy," performed by the band, then Something new: "Amor" from the then current 1944 film *Broadway Rhythm*, sung by Bing; Something borrowed: from Harry James "Music Makers" and Something Blue, "Farewell Blues."

Bing, Jerry Gray and Glenn
(courtesy Kathryn Crosby)

Bing and the singing, swinging Crew Chiefs vocal group took over performing "Swinging on a Star" from Bing's 1944 film *Going My Way* accompanied by the Uptown Hall small group from within the Miller band, consisting of leader Mel Powell, piano; Bernie Privin, trumpet; Peanuts Hucko, clarinet; Ray McKinley drums; Carmen Mastren, guitar; and Trigger Albert on the string bass, all arranged by Jerry Gray.

The Crew Chiefs and Bing kneaded voices on the beautiful ballad "Poinciana," the session being capped instrumentally with Glenn's immortal theme "Moonlight Serenade."

The date of this famous, live broadcast/recording session was Thursday, August 31, 1944, lasting from 8:30 til 9:00 p.m. at the Paris Cinema in London, England, with about 300 servicemen and women attending, all very happy to be entertained by Glenn Miller, Bing Crosby and the band.

Bing: *"Glenn, thanks for letting me hitch a ride on your high flying half hour. I hope to see more of you fighting guys out there soon. So long for now, I'll be getting around to see you."*

After the recording session, Bing took off a hand-painted tie he was wearing and autographed it to "Glenn Miller's AAF Band—the Greatest Thing Since the Invention of Cup Mutes!"

The boys in the band were mutually impressed with Bing's lack of formality, a contrast to Miller's usual disciplined attitude. The band members took home fond memories of the Crosby session. Bing had brought some hard-to-find bottles of scotch and rye for the musicians. It was said on that day the band had recorded some of their best material ever.

A fog rolled in on them that night, Bing remembered: "We had to crawl back to our hotel about a mile on our hands and knees, feeling the curb as we moved along.

"I was going to France in a day or so, and Glenn offered to send his pianist, Jack Russin, over to expand my accompaniment. He left on a later plane, and though he got to France, we never did get together."

Mark Scrimger: "Well, this ended 40 years of speculation over this broadcast's recording alleged existence.

Impossible as it may seem, this is the only known recording of Bing singing with the Glenn Miller Orchestra. Their paths never crossed, Bing being anchored to Decca Records and Glenn contracted tightly to RCA. Sadly, this turned out to be their final meeting. Together they did their bit to boost morale and entertain the war-weary people of the British Isles and were able to reach the fighting men in Europe through the transcription broadcast. At the time, the Glenn Miller Orchestra and Bing Crosby were probably the most popular entertainers in show business, especially with respect to recorded music."

Earlier, before Glenn folded his civilian band, he approached Bing for a letter of recommendation when he applied for a job with the Army Air Force where he wanted to form a military band to entertain the troops here and overseas. Bing sent the a letter praising the bandleader, and Glenn got the job.

who didn't love and appreciate the music of Glenn Miller, to which I was a great listener.

"As a person, Glenn was as memorable as his music. He was a good, personal friend. He had innate class and taste. He loved good things—musically and in his personal life.

"I have no doubt, had he lived, he would have been a tremendous force in popular music in the ensuing years."

Skip Nelson
Scipione Mirabella

When vocalist Ray Eberle left Glenn's band just before it disbanded, Skip Martin, who also played piano and guitar, was fortunate to record with Glenn as a vocalist on two of the best Glenn Miller recordings, "That Old Black Magic," his very first recording, and in collaboration with the Modernaires, and "Dearly Beloved," two among the final recordings made for RCA Victor in the nick of time just before the infamous recording strike. With those two records, Skip Nelson secured himself a permanent place in the Glenn Miller library of great hits.

Beryl Davis
Major Glenn Miller's Last Lady Vocalist

Beryl tells the story that in the year 2000 she was with the BBC at Twinwood Farm, Bedford, England, making a video tape of her signature song "I'll Be Seeing You." It was pouring rain, windy and cold. She alighted from the small building with her producer and cameraman, when a middle aged couple ambled up to them as Beryl was getting in her car, and inquired what she was doing there—in the couples farm building, that is.

"That couple had no clue that it was the very airfield building from which Glenn Miller left in that single engine plane heading for Paris on his fatal trip." They turned out to be the owners of Twinwood Farm there in Bedford. They are now the

Tommy Dorsey and Beryl Davis - 1947
(courtesy Beryl Davis)

people who turned the neglected airport property around, establishing a museum and constructing an arena to help celebrate that infamous day, December 15, 1944, that has become an annual event."

Looking back a bit to that time:

ON NOVEMBER 2, 1944,
A COMMUNIQUÉ WAS
ISSUED FROM LIEUTENANT
GENERAL JIMMY DOOLITTLE
AT THE EIGHTH AIR FORCE
HEADQUARTERS

The communiqué outlined invitational travel orders to a pretty young British singer as an authority for providing entertainment at air force installations in England. The excited young lady was London born Beryl Davis. Beryl was the only British civilian ever attached to the American 8th Air Force.

Beryl Davis and I have worked together many times in the past. The most recent when I profiled her in my book "Jukebox Saturday Night," published in 1998, and before when her old friends, legendary big band vocalist Connie Haines, who sang shoulder to shoulder with Frank Sinatra in Tommy Dorsey's band back in the forties, and superstars Jane Russell and Rhonda Fleming, all appeared together in my biography of Connie Haines, *Snootie Little Cutie*.

Beryl's father was a bandleader in London and she would sing with his band when she was a mere eight years old. She performed in music halls all over England, Scotland and Wales, anywhere her father would travel with his troupe. On cue, she would hop up on stage and sing a rousing chorus of "Constantinople," collect a box of chocolates and then run offstage to smiles and applause, all while her father was leading the pit band.

"All the American singers were my musical heroes. I listened to the Big Bands all the time because it was the only way I could learn the songs, particularly when the war came. We were isolated, and perhaps would get just one record a month, and everybody would run to the music store to find a new song. We did Glenn Miller and Tommy Dorsey stuff. I would listen on my little wind-up phonograph to Ella Fitzgerald, Helen O'Connell, Helen Forrest, Maxine Sullivan, and Connie Haines."

Beryl's career blossomed throughout the war and she became England's prominent vocalist. "I sang with Syd Lawrence, Mantovani, and Ted Heath, all the great English bands. In Paris, during the war, I performed with Belgian gypsy guitarist Django Reinhardt and jazz violinist Stephane Grappelli in a small group that included [blind pianist] George Shearing. It was, musically speaking, the most wonderful time of my life."

With bombs falling around them, Beryl just learned to handle the pressure, running from door to door in an air raid. The daily bombings were a way of life, so she was never terrified. Then, Glenn Miller came to town with his powerhouse Army Air Force Band.

> *"I was very excited about that, because, for me, that was the creme-de-la-creme of bands. Glenn had the Crew Chiefs and Johnny Desmond, and I was invited to join because I had an American sound, accent, and knew all those Glenn Miller charts. Glenn was a quiet, elegant and very much a leader."*

Beryl became the number one favorite girl singer of American Forces overseas. The very last show she performed with the Glenn Miller Orchestra was at the Queensbury Club, on Lower Regent Street in the heart of London, on December 12, 1944. She sang the haunting war song "I'll Be Seeing You."

"As Glenn left, he patted me on the shoulder, and said, 'Good show, kid! I'll be seeing you.'"

After Glenn was lost, Beryl decided to expand her career and emigrate to America. She always wanted to go, but only for the music and no other reason. She wanted to meet Nat "King" Cole, Frank Sinatra, and all her other musical heroes. And she did! When Bob Hope heard her recording of "I'll Be Seeing You," he had Willard Alexander, who booked all the big band acts at the time with his Alexander Agency, bring her to Hollywood to debut on his radio show.

Beryl sang with Frank Sinatra on *Your Hit Parade* radio show, replacing Doris Day, who was headed for a movie career performing in her first film *Romance on the High Seas*.

Later, Beryl met and married Peter Potter, famous Hollywood disc jockey, and had three children. Joining with Connie Haines, Jane Russell and Rhonda Fleming, they recorded "Do Lord," a record that went gold. All members of the same Hollywood church, they toured and performed on the shows of Bob Hope, Red Skelton, and Ed Sullivan, and was featured on the Abbott & Costello, Milton Berle, and Hedda Hopper radio shows.

"I also sang with Kay Kyser's band and, over the years, on many salutes to Glenn Miller." Beryl was later married to Buck Stapleton, whom she recently lost. Buck was, ironically, a member of Glenn's Air Force Band, and later a promotion manager for Capitol Records.

Beryl performed at the Twinwood Reunion in August of 2003, singing with the British Glenn Miller Orchestra under the direction of Ray McVay, who is also featured in this book, having been interviewed by Swiss disc jockey Max Wirz in October, 2003.

"Richard, there were thousands of people there in that field who came to listen to Glenn's great music. It was amazing. I was so proud to be a part of it. Lately, I do my thing about Glenn on cruise ships, preceded by a talking performance by the great Glenn Miller musician, Paul Tanner. He is always there telling everyone about Glenn and his music and how it was back then."

Beryl has never been, or will ever be, just an observer. She is still a vital part of the music scene. Her rendition of "I'll Be Seeing You" has become her vocal trademark and is always dedicated to the memory of Major Glenn Miller.

Connie Haines, Jane Russell, Beryl Davis and Rhonda Fleming

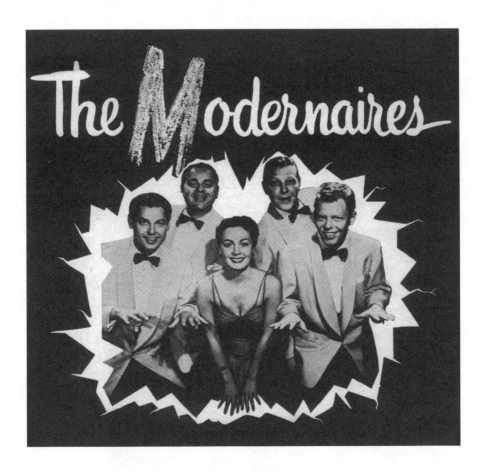

The "Mods" Modernaires

When Glenn was adding more musicians to his band he extended it even further, experimenting with a singing group known as the *Modernaires*, whose spokesman was Hal Dickenson.

"The first time we did anything with Glenn was recording the theme for WNEW disc jockey Martin Block. It was entitled "It's Make Believe Ballroom Time," and was recorded on

The Modernaires at the Waldorf - 1950
Fran Scot, Hal Dickinson, Paula Kelly Dickinson, Johnny Drake and Allan Copeland.
(courtesy Metronome Magazine)

October 11, 1940. And, that's where Glenn first got the idea that he wanted to have a quartet singing with his band.And, just a few recording sessions later, we became an official part of the Glenn Miller organization for good."

On Christmas day of 1940, the Modernaires stepped into New York's Pennsylvania Hotel, located the beautiful

Cafe Rouge, and sat down there in their raggedy clothes. Observing the band in rehearsal, they were awe stricken by the hearty, twangy vocals of Tex Beneke, and were mesmerized by the musical excellence of the number one band in the world, a band who had just won the coveted "Billboard" listeners poll.

"The fact that we were going to appear with the band was almost breathtaking. Glenn bought us dinner. If we'd have known that in advance, we would have had something more expensive to eat. We officially joined with the band in 1941. At the first session we performed a Jimmy Van Heusen song, 'You stepped out of a dream.'"

"The original Modernaires were a group of four musical guys with diverse backgrounds from Buffalo, New York. Hal Dickenson was the lead singer and a Presbyterian; Ralph Brewster, a Christian Scientist who played trumpet; Chuck Goldstein was a Jew, and Bill Conway was a Catholic, who also played guitar. None of them read music. They sang and played, as they say, strictly by ear.

Chuck Goldstein: "Hal was the lead singer, but could only sing the melody. I could sing both upper and lower harmony. Bill would sit with his guitar and we would learn our songs working together in our own special harmony. And we made pretty good money, getting a hundred and twenty-five bucks each, plus bonus."

The "Mods" had been working with Paul "Pops" Whiteman, who graciously allowed them to tear up their contract in order for them to join up with Glenn. Glenn felt the presence of a vocal group would attract customers around the bandstand enabling people to stand eye-to-eye with both players and vocalists.

Aside from the great hits "Chattanooga Choo Choo," "Don't Sit Under the Apple Tree" and "Kalamazoo," the "Mods" introduced with Glenn Miller, they also produced the beautiful ballad "Perfidia," with Dorothy Claire, "You Stepped Out of a Dream," with Ray Eberle, "Sweeter Than the Sweetest," with Paula Kelly, "Booglie Wooglie Piggy," also with Paula Kelly and Tex Beneke, as well as "I Know Why," one of Glenn's greatest hits, also with Paula Kelly. Of course, the hits came through the years until the disbanding of Glenn's civilian band in September of 1942.

Billy May arranged specifically for the Modernaires from time to time.

"When the Mods wanted to do something other than backing up the featured singers, they came up with 'Sweeter Than The Sweetest,' so I made a special arrangement for them. Chuck Goldstein and Hal Dickinson and I were never really happy with that arrangement, but Glenn was in a hurry to get it to the recording studio. I think it could have been even better. With Glenn, you know, the band was always very well rehearsed and everything was marked. There was no need to conduct the band because it always was so well rehearsed. So with great arrangements and strong rehearsals, the band didn't need anyone standing up there waving a baton."

Bill Finegan: "Usually, we worked the vocal parts out with the Modernaires, and in some cases we would write out the voice parts before we did the whole arrangement. But, we went both ways with that. Besides singing with the group, Bill Conway was then the brains of the Modernaires and we would work with Bill."

Today's Modernaires are known as the *Moonlight Serenaders*. Some playing members of Larry O'Brien's current crop of musicians double up as vocalists. Matt Johns, James Borowski, and Kevin Sheehan, along with band vocalists Nick Hilscher and Julia Rich, combine to share the spotlight as the *Moonlight Serenaders*. And, do they ever perform so beautifully. You could close your eyes and appreciate their interpretation of the original charts with full orchestral backing, transporting you back a few years, evoking the sounds of the original Modernaires.

Johnny Desmond

Glenn's wartime orchestra was large and magnificent. There were over forty service men in the band. Recruit Johnny Desmond acquired his singing job with the band by the simple means of writing Glenn a letter asking him to consider selecting him. Desmond was only a lad of twenty-four.

Johnny: "The day I sent a letter to him, he was building a band of good musicians. He called for me and it was that easy.

"Under Glenn's guidance I developed a unique, personal vocal style that the fans really liked. That started off my long, fifty year career."

Giovanni Alfredo Desimons came to first light in Detroit, Michigan, studied at the city's Music Conservatory, and worked local radio shows as an actor and vocalized in local night clubs. He organized a vocal group, called the Downbeats, which came to the attention of bandleader Bob Crosby when his band played through Detroit. Crosby, Bing's brother, changed the name of the vocal group to the Bob-O-Links who remained with the band for a year or so.

Johnny sang briefly with Gene Krupa's swinging band before he was drafted and joined up with Glenn's AAF Orchestra where he sang on many of the broadcasts in England. Johnny went to Paris and remained for six months until the outfit disbanded in November of 1945. Johnny Desmond continued his career as a soloist upon returning to civilian life. He was booked for a radio show, eventually signing a recording contract with RCA Victor.

Johnny Desmond played piano, was a capable dancer and songwriter, and appeared with Barbra Streisand on Broadway in *Funny Girl*. Naturally, Johnny was invited to appear at various Glenn Miller reunions through the years.

Some fans and critics compared Johnny to Frank Sinatra, although his phrasing and voicing was really different, sounding perhaps more like Dick Haymes, but his voice was always crisp and clear. His recording of "My Heart Tells

Me" is a fine example. So is "All through the Night" and "I Love You" recorded in England with the Glenn Miller Allied Expeditionery Force Orchestra in 1944.

Johnny Desmond

The Bandleaders and Bookers

Harry James Takes The Chesterfield Spotlight

Glenn Transfers His Baton to Harry James on the Chesterfield Radio Broadcasts

On October 24, 1942, bandleader Harry James sat in one of the trumpet chairs to perform with the Glenn Miller Orchestra on their Chesterfield radio program, *Moonlight Serenade*. For Glenn and the orchestra it was a night for farewells. For the Harry James band it was a night to celebrate appearances on a newly acquired engagement that would help promote his fledgling band. Harry was chosen by Glenn to perform with Glenn's immensely successful civilian orchestra on their final radio program.

Glenn speaks to Harry James following the bands swinging rendition of "Jukebox Saturday Night."

Glenn: "That was 'Jukebox Saturday Night,' and that man imitating Harry James did a good job. The reason—because that was Harry James himself. Harry, come on over here and say something."

(applause)
Harry: "Well, hello everybody!"

(more applause)

Glenn: "Harry, naturally, we are very reluctant to give up our *Moonlight Serenade* show, but since I've got a date with Uncle Sam coming up, I can sincerely say that I would rather you take over our regular Tuesday, Wednesday and Thursday spot on this radio show, than any one I know. So, next Tuesday—get to work, Mister."

Harry: "O.K. Captain Miller—that sounds like an order. But, seriously, Glenn, I'm sure everyone will agree with me that you're doing a mighty fine thing going in the army."

Glenn: "Thank you very much, Harry. You know, it makes me feel a little sad to leave Marion, Tex, Skip, the Modernaires, and this wonderful gang of boys in the band and all our friends listening. There's a lot of swell guys in the outfit I'm going in, and maybe all of us can get together again after this thing is over. In the meantime, I'll see you all in the army and we'll say goodbye."

Of course, Harry James needs no introduction. Most people seem to remember Harry James and his band from appearances in those splashy, glitzy 1940s movies, *Springtime in the Rockies* and *Best Foot Forward*, and the fact that he was married to World War II's most popular pinup, Betty Grable, "The girl with the world's most beautiful legs," who also starred in those films.

Harry James and I talked about his career in 1981 in Northport High School's backstage dressing room on Long Island.

"I was at the Brooklyn Paramount when I first started, and Frank Sinatra was singing at a little place called the Rustic Cabin near Alpine, New Jersey, and I used to hear him on a local radio show when I was driving home, but didn't know who he was because they didn't say. We needed two things—a vocalist and a boost for the band, and we got both. Connie Haines and I went to see him and we hired him on the spot." He had just hired Connie and was on the way home

Connie and Frank
(Connie Haines collection)

from Philadelphia, where Connie first sang with the band. Harry's other break was when WNEW disc jockey Martin Block continually played Harry's recording of "You Made Me Love You" on his *Make Believe Ballroom* radio show making it an instant hit in New York. However, Harry was not aware of this and when he arrived from Philadelphia with the band for an appearance at the Brooklyn Paramount, he was shocked to see hundreds of people in line at the theater.

> *"When we got there about eight in the morning, we wondered what was happening—did somebody kill someone—was there a fire, or something? Somebody said, 'Are you kidding? We are waiting to see Harry James.' So I said, 'How come?' and he says, 'Martin Block has been playing the 'You Made Me Love You' single for the last two weeks on the* Make Believe Ballroom *show and it made the song and the band had a hit."*

The record sold 2.5 million copies. It ended two lean years for the fledgling bandleader and his players. Both Frank Sinatra and Connie Haines were the featured singers in the band, and after Sinatra left to go to Tommy Dorsey, Dick Haymes took his place on the bandstand. I enjoyed the story Harry James told me about his two, new Selmer trumpets, when he was playing trumpet with Benny Goodman.

"We were on our way to Hollywood to film Hollywood Hotel, *and I got off the bus with my case under my arm to board the Los Angles Limited train. But, I forgot my jacket. I put down the double case and I went back on the bus, and the bus decided to backup and the wheels turned and ran over the case with the trumpets inside. It flattened them like a pancake."*
  "What did you do?"
  "I cried!"

And we both laughed. Fortunately, Benny Goodman bought Harry two new Selmers when they arrived in L.A. Harry James was, what Ray Anthony once told me, "The Best Damn Trumpet Player," which became the title of my first book in 1996.

Willard Alexander
Big Band Salesman

In 1934, young Willard Alexander, a bright "band booker" who was working for MCA (Music Corporation of America) representing and launching the "sweet" bands of Wayne King, Sammy Kaye, Horace Heidt and Guy Lombardo, crossed over to work for an equally large and aggressive talent agency named William Morris, (up to then a mostly vaudeville and nightclub star agency).

There, he initiated a big band department and developed a creative and efficient group, handling such veterans as Duke Ellington, Paul Whiteman, Count Basie, Glenn Miller,

Willard Alexander and Richard Grudens
Westbury, NY - 1983

Vaughn Monroe, and bravely took on numerous new and untried *avant-garde* musical organizations like those of Dizzy Gillespie, Billy Eckstine, and Charlie Spivak. He brought them to the attention of the public through strategic bookings in theaters, pavilions and night clubs all over the United States. Dizzy stayed six years, eventually forming his own, Willard Alexander Agency Inc.of Madison Avenue, New York, with satellite offices in Chicago, Beverly Hills, and London. He consistently represented the cream of the music industry.

One evening in 1983 I met up with Willard Alexander backstage at Westbury Music Fair on Long Island where he had booked Larry O'Brien and the Glenn Miller Orchestra, whom he presently represented. We sat together on a two-man bench in the hallway adjacent to the dressing rooms listening to Dizzy Gillespie telling his famous stories to anyone who would listen. He had dropped in to visit his friend, Billy Eckstine, who was singing with Larry O'Brien and the Glenn Miller Orchestra that night, along with singer Margaret Whiting.

"I guess you've been through this kind of thing a thousand or so times," I said.

"Oh, sure, and I am still doing it. It's the work I have always loved."

Willard practiced the tradition of attending the opening night of any band he personally booked, no matter where, and this engagement was no exception. It was legendary booker Willard Alexander who represented the great Benny Goodman at the event of the revolutionary 1938 Carnegie Hall Jazz Concert, the first such concert in the famed music hall.

"Willard, that had to be quite a feat, to get a popular jazz band to play Carnegie Hall where only serious classical music was performed."

"Believe it or not, it was very easy to make bookings for jazz bands. They were becoming in great demand. The world was ready for Benny by that time. We thought he was known well enough to try it. In those days there were very few concert halls—no Avery Fisher or Lincoln Center, you know. When you get as big and as hot and confident as Goodman was in those days, why not? We felt we had a winner...and we were right. Filling 2,800 seats was no great thing for a concert hall."

Fabled impresario Sol Hurok had helped plan the concert with his services and handling the publicity, telling the world that modern jazz would be played at Carnegie Hall for the first time, while Willard actually booked the hall. Hurok's name carried a lot of weight in the field, although it was also his first jazz concert. Willard and I continued to articulate jazz history, his involvement with Glenn Miller, and about subsequent leaders of Glenn's great band. Willard Alexander came from the old school. A perfect, dignified gentleman from an earlier time with a white, oxford button-down shirt and a polka dot tie.

The Big Bands, like that of the Glenn Miller Orchestra and others, have to thank dedicated men like Willard Alexander who promoted and booked the bands into the great hotels, pavilions and theaters of America and helped make them the great musical organizations they became during the Big Band Era and beyond.

CELEBRATION

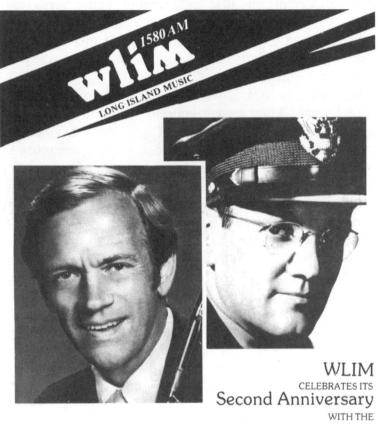

1580 AM
wlim
LONG ISLAND MUSIC

WLIM
CELEBRATES ITS
Second Anniversary
WITH THE
The Glenn Miller Band
FEATURING
Larry O'Brien
FOR THE BENEFIT OF
THAW
TALENTED HANDICAPPED ARTISTS WORKSHOP

KNIGHTS OF COLUMBUS HALL
PATCHOGUE, NEW YORK
SUNDAY, JULY 17, 1983

Larry O'Brien

Perspective with Glenn Miller Orchestra Director, Larry O'Brien

> *"Glenn Miller's music may just live forever. Glenn's music is like finely machined tools—all the parts fit perfectly."*

Those words from today's Glenn Miller Orchestra director Larry O'Brien were told to me one summer evening back in 1982 when Larry and I were backstage talking with world famous big band booker Willard Alexander, who was present that night at the Westbury Music Fair on Long Island where the orchestra he booked was performing in a show featuring WNEW's legendary radio host William B. Williams, and famed vocalists Margaret Whiting and Billy Eckstine.

So, how did Larry O'Brien come to direct the most famous big band in the world was the question I extended to Willard Alexander:

"Larry was working at the Dunes in Las Vegas and I had my people approach him to lead the Miller band. Larry was

Larry O'Brien and Jack Ellsworth - 1983
(Jack Ellsworth collection)

working for the Dorsey organization led by Sam Donohue and a house band in Vegas. I forgot what brought Larry to my attention. Anyway, we recommended him. We felt he would keep in tune, so to speak, with the Miller sound, and he looked darn good as a leader."

According to Larry, here's the story on how he captured the coveted Glenn Miller appointment?

"As far as I know, they invited me to lead the Glenn Miller band probably because of my experience with the Tommy Dorsey band and conducting with Frank Sinatra, Jr. That lit up a lamp in somebody's head. So I was called and offered the job.

I said, 'Yeah! I'll take it,' and then David Mackay called me, talked further, then came out to Vegas to watch me play and sealed the deal. David Mackay, who was Glenn's close friend, attorney, and executor of his estate, owned the worldwide rights to license the use of the Glenn Miller name and music book, or charts, as they are referred to in the business.

His son, David Mackay, Jr. carries on the tradition today."

Larry was greatly surprised to even be considered, realizing that for him it was a major step. Flattered and mildly apprehensive, knowing he was following some very fine leaders, Larry hoped he would be able to uphold the Glenn Miller Orchestra's tradition.

Earlier, Larry had played in many of the famous big bands during the sixties: Ray McKinley's Glenn Miller Orchestra, Sammy Kaye, Buddy Morrow, who still directs the Tommy Dorsey big band today, Lee Castle, Art Mooney, and Ralph Marterie, being regularly featured as trombone soloist on all the Dorsey solos. He had spent some years as leader of a group backing Frank Sinatra, Jr. in appearances and on recordings.

Larry's introduction to the world of music occurred the day his dad, a craftsman who could create most anything with his hands, fashioned him a pretty good homemade violin in the kitchen of their Ozone Park, New York home. Larry was ten.

> *"He placed it on the kitchen table. But, the violin was not for me. I wanted to play the trombone, especially when I heard a friend practicing on one in the rear of his dad's dry cleaning shop. My dad obviously could not make one for me, so I had to get one, myself. It had to wait until I got into John Adams High School where I borrowed one while taking lessons at school."*

Then, Larry received advanced lessons from his technically excellent teacher, Eddie Collier, an older, fellow high school alumni who was playing in Broadway shows pit bands. At sixteen, Larry won the New York Philharmonic Scholarship and *made* the prestigious All-City School Orchestra. He began his big band career playing a very smooth trombone in the house band at the Frontier Hotel in Las Vegas, backing various big-name acts who were performing as part of the Vegas star policy of the time.

Later on, in 1996, Larry and I talked once again about the future of the Miller Orchestra, saying, "It's amazing. The applause is still tremendous today. Those tunes bring back a lot of memories. For example, we do

Larry, Connie Haines, Richard Grudens
Stonybrook, NY - 2002
(Ben Grisafi photo)

'That Old Black Magic' and 'People Like You and Me,' in addition to the regular stuff."

But, even then, Larry confirmed, "In the Mood" and "Moonlight Serenade" along with "Chattanooga Choo Choo" remain the top requested tunes at concerts.

Now old friends, Larry and I got together once again in 2001 when he attended a book signing and luncheon I hosted for big band vocalist Connie Haines at the old Three Village Inn in Stonybrook, New York. A true fan of Connie's, Larry, fortunately, had the band circulating close by and was able to steal away a few hours to attend, much to Connie's delight. His good news was that he had just re-signed to direct the orchestra for three more years. Larry and I were destined to meet one more time in preparation for this book. It was at the Westhampton Beach Performing Arts Center in late July 2003, which is profiled in the chapter detailing today's Glenn Miller Orchestra.

Glenn — A Word or Two About Tom Sheils

Glenn Miller had a number of people he depended upon during his mercurial rise to fame with his second band. An important one was Tom Sheils who secured the original engagement at the Glen Island Casino that followed the engagement at the Meadowbrook. Tom lived close to, and knew the management of, the prestigious Glen Island venue in New Rochelle, New York, and persuaded them to check out Glenn's performances at the Paradise Restaurant. They promptly signed Glenn for the 1939 Summer Season at the Glen Island Casino, a critical booking leading to the band's great success.

Tom was also responsible for an earlier booking for the band directly after the Paradise Restaurant engagement, a relief for the band that enabled Glenn to meet his weekly payroll. Being indebted to Tom and ultimately utilizing his skills in the booking business, Gloenn hired Tom to represent the band.

As John Tumpak, noted Big Band Historian wrote in a recent 2004 article in L.A. Jazz Scene: "Miller now had the hottest band in the country, thanks in part to the assistance of Tom Sheils, Glenn Miller's right hand man."

According to Tumpak, Paul Tanner added: There is no doubt that Tom Sheils played an important part in helping us land the Glen Island Casino engagement in 1939. By the time we closed in August you couldn't find a parking spot. Playing there put us over the top. By that alone Tom deserves a solid place in Glenn Miller history."

Tom became good friends with Chummy MacGregor and Hal McIntyre, also close friends of Glenn. Tom remained with the orchestra right through its closing in September of 1942, during which time he produced radio shows, and subsequently handled all Glenn's contracts before and after the civilian band disbanded.

It was Tom who was present when Helen Miller received notice from the war department that Glenn was missing in flight.

Tom contends that Glenn had a myriad of plans for his return to civilian life after the war. "He had planned to open up a big time booking agency with his band heading it up, and that he planned to expand his music publishing company, Mutual Music, and to continue representing talent. Glenn also said he had a standing offer from Coca-Cola to do a one hour radio show."

Tom Sheils continued to represent talent: The Modernaires, Carmel Quinn, Johnny Carson, the DeCastro Sisters, Jimmy Dean, Mike Douglas, Tex Beneke, among others, until he retired.

In March, 2002, Tom hosted a tribute to Glenn at the Wellington Retirement Community in Laguna Hills, California, with the help of Alan Cass, curator of the Glenn Miller Archives at the University of Colorado, and Jonnie Dee Miller, Glenn's daughter, Billy May and Dr. Paul Tanner.

1944-1956 INTERLUDE

The state of Glenn's band from December 1944 through 1956 before David Mackay formed Glenn Miller Productions.

Immediately after Glenn's disappearance, Ray McKinley became the natural heir to directing the Air Force band.

The bands first performance, after Glenn was lost, was held on December 21, 1944 at the Palaies de Glace, solely for troops on limited leave. The band played at Red Cross and Enlisted Men's club venues in Paris and at special request locations. By May of 1945, the orchestra was playing in Germany under the direction of General Omar Bradley, and then for a tremendous audience of 40,000 Allied troops at giant Nuremberg Stadium.

The entire band returned to the States on August 12, 1945.

Glenn's Air Force band's final appearance occurred at the National Press Club in Washington, D.C. in front of President Harry Truman and future President General Dwight D. Eisenhower.

For a limited engagement, Jerry Gray directed the band on NBC's radio program *I Sustain the Wings*, composed of mostly Glenn Miller alumnus. But it was Tex Beneke whom Helen Miller and David Mackay, Sr. eventually chose to lead the post-war Glenn Miller civilian orchestra, composed of about 40 musicians and vocalists. Gradually, Tex Beneke changed the band to reflect his own name and invoked his own musical arrangments, and by the end of 1950, broke with Miller and Mackay and went exclusively on his own.

Other bands cashed in, simulating Glenn's great sound, including Ralph Flanagan, Ray Anthony, and Jerry Gray. At the time, however, beginning in 1953, RCA began releasing collections of Glenn's recordings. The albums succeeded and spawned the film *The Glenn Miller Story*, thanks to David Mackay's untiring efforts.

In 1956, Helen Miller and David Mackay recalled to life a new wave of Glenn Miller Orchestras invoking Glenn's entire library of original charts. On April 6, 1956, under the baton of Ray McKinley, the official Glenn Miller Orchestra was back in business and continues to this day.

THE GLENN MILLER ORCHESTRA
BANDLEADERS THROUGH 2003

Ray McKinley
June 6, 1956 - January 5, 1966

Ray became the first new leader of the Glenn Miller Orchestra and had a successful ten year run.

Back in the old days, before Glenn's band was first formed, vocalist Smith Ballew had a fine band, and when he performed the vocal on "Blues Serenade," a recording

made in 1935 with his band, Ballew placed the name of Glenn Miller on the label as leader. Glenn, of course, was a trombone player and did arranging for the band. Drummer Ray McKinley was also in that band and on that record date. Those were the depression years and everyone was trying to keep body and soul together.

Ray: "We would skip from one hotel band to another. Glenn was always there, and then Glenn took five of us from that band and brought us into the Dorsey's, and later into the Ray Noble Band which he helped get started."

Ray had started his own short-lived band in 1940. Big band agent, Willard Alexander, had booked the band into many fine venues like the Famous Door on 52nd Street and the Paramount Theater on Broadway, both in New York City. Will Bradley fronted the band, as he and Ray were financial partners. The partnership self-destructed, the two leaders going in opposite directions. In 1942, Ray continued on his own until the draft of World War II reduced the availability of players and eventually enlisted Ray himself. There, he joined up with Glenn once again in the Army Air Force Band at Yale University.

Ray McKinley: "At Yale, in New Haven, Connecticut, where Glenn organized all of us into a full-blown band, we would march up and down the vast green to play retreat each day. Kids on bicycles would peddle along with the band and we drummed out, or played something like 'Buckle Down Winsocki.' We tried playing the 'St Louis Blues' that we neatly turned into a march. The guys would've otherwise gone crazy with playing rumpt-teh-dumpt over and over. So we played that tune that was structured perfectly for a march. It was all drums and brass. No reeds at all. Later, RCA recorded it and it became a big hit when Tex Beneke recorded it with the first postwar Miller band. "Ray became a key player with Glenn in the Air Force Band."

In 1944, at the height of the war, when the band went to England, the endless appearances, record sessions, and live broadcasts, kept Ray McKinley and the band extremely busy.

"It was hard, all right. From early morning 'til sometimes midnight, we'd get in a plane and fly from one base to another. The brass section was worn out. It was the hardest time I had in the music business, but we did it for the guys and gals who needed our support. We did our job."

The last Army Air Force concert in England was performed at the Queensbury All-Services Club on December 12, 1944. Morton Downey was a guest vocalist, and the Marquess of Queensbury hosted a dinner for everyone after the show.

After the infamous date of December 15, 1944, when the world lost Glenn Miller, drummer Ray McKinley became the driving force behind the Glenn Miller Army Air Force Band as it's leader for the remaining eight month European tour. Ray led the great dance band and fought for its rights with Army brass, winning the respect and affection of its soldier-musicians.

After World War II, Ray started his own organization in 1946, that, again, never really succeeded. The band boasted some great musicians: saxist "Peanuts" Hucko, guitarist Mundell Lowe, trumpeter Chuck Genduso, pianist Lou Stein, trombonist Irv Dinkin, saxist Deane Kincaide, with arrangements by Kincaide and Eddie Sauter. Ray performed his own vocals.

From 1956 to 1966, after Tex Beneke gave up the Glenn Miller baton in favor of his own Tex Beneke band, Ray was signed by the Miller estate to lead the still popular Glenn Miller Orchestra and became forever identified deeply with Glenn's music while keeping Glenn's famous sound alive. Ray kept the familiar clarinet lead and the *ooh-wahs* of the brass in the arrangements, but some McKinley stuff slipped in here and there.

"The Memorial albums had just come out and made a lot of money for the estate and Victor, and the Glenn Miller movie enjoyed great success, first time around. Not too many years after that, Willard Alexander got a hold of David Mackay, the attorney for the estate, and suggested that they rejuvenate a Glenn Miller Orchestra and use the library and the name and all that. They had to go to Helen Miller for permission, of course. She was alive then, but she said that depends on who you are going to have lead it. When they said Ray McKinley, why she remembered me from the old days kicking around, when in the hotels we were so hard up that we put the dirty clothes in the bathtub and threw in a lot of soap, and got in there and walked around on them. So, she said. 'That's fine, yes, go straight ahead.' So, we did."

After ten successful years, and experiencing the weariness that comes with traveling across the country and around the world with the band, Ray McKinley turned the baton over to clarinetist Buddy De Franco, and retired from leading a band. Ray was easily able to procure more lucrative and reasonable work in television and radio.

Buddy De Franco
January 6, 1966 - January 17, 1974

When 80 year old (February 2004) Buddy De Franco soloed on Tommy Dorsey's original recording of "Opus One," everyone got to know his fine work. Buddy's reputation as an impressive jazz clarinetist has followed him from the days of the Swing Era right into the present. In-between, Buddy directed the official Glenn Miller Orchestra immediately following Ray McKinley's tenure and held it for some eight years, until 1974.

Buddy was merely nine years old when he began work on his clarinet, and in 1941, at age fourteen, he won a national Tommy Dorsey swing contest and appeared on a radio show with Gene Krupa. Later, he joined Gene's band. In 1950, after some stellar work with other bands, including Tommy Dorsey, Buddy became a player in the Count Basie Septet.

Living in Florida now, Buddy DeFranco is promoting a new CD with the Jay Patten Swing Orchestra. Jay was a guitar player in the Miller band and even sang with the band. He is now a top arranger and has his own orchestra.

Buddy talked readily about his old association with the Glenn Miller Orchestra.

"Working the Glenn Miller years, I had charts by Bill Finegan and Jerry Gray that were superior. I thought Glenn's music a bit commercial, but the framework was just fantastic. We were able to breathe new and fresh ideas into the Miller category. We tried with some of the lesser known charts that did not become as popular. After a while, I was able to slip about twenty minutes of jazz in my programs. My fans wanted to hear that and it was a good balance."

Buddy DeFranco's vision of the future includes faith in better music that he feels is forthcoming, thanks to better trained and more dedicated musicians appearing on the horizon. Schools and their musical directors, which have swing bands, are keeping the music going.

As Tony Bennett would say, "It's not old music, it's good music, and good music will always prevail over bad music.

"Rock and rap is considered entertainment and has never had anything to do with music. Music was just a part of it; that wasn't the focal point. Jazz and Big Bands and Swing music will survive. Just listen to the current Glenn Miller group of musicians to prove the point."

Buddy is considered to be the world's number one clarinet player. He has won an unprecedented twenty *Downbeat Magazine Awards*, as well as awards by Playboy all-stars polls and Metronome Magazine contests.

Michael Andrew "Peanuts" Hucko
January 18, 1974 - September 16, 1974

Peanuts Hucko has enjoyed a fine musical reputation for many years, from the days he played tenor sax with Will Bradley's and Joe Marsala's band before World War II, and Charlie Spivak's shortly afterwards. He joined Glenn's Army Air Force band, with which he often performed as a clarinet soloist.

John Miller and Peanuts Hucko at Pontin's Pakefield, England.
(John Miller collection)

He played in many big bands including touring with Benny Goodman, playing with Jack Teagarden, and in the Louis Armstrong All Stars from 1958 through 1960. And, of course, his appearances on the Lawrence Welk television shows made him a popular musical celebrity. After his Glenn Miller director experience, Peanuts opened a nightclub in Denver, Colorado, featuring Louise Tobin, his wife, as vocalist. Peanuts capped his career in the 1980's with his own Pied Piper Quartet.

Peanuts Hucko's musical voice was silenced just a few weeks ago from this writing in August, 2003.

Buddy Morrow
September 17, 1974 - March 30, 1975

Buddy Morrow and I go back to the early 1980's when he was first leading the Tommy Dorsey Orchestra. I met with him for a series of interviews for a show business magazine. Did you know that Buddy's real name is Moe (Muni) Zudekoff.

Buddy Morrow and Richard Grudens, 1983
(Camille Smith photo)

Of course you don't. (It's really not a secret.) He coined the name "Buddy Morrow" in the early 1940's while a studio musician.

Buddy hides his handsome face behind a signature beard. His experience was playing in the great bands of Paul Whiteman, Artie Shaw and Tommy Dorsey, but it was Bunny Berigan of "I Can't Get Started" fame, who recognized his talent and recommended him to Shaw.

After a short period of trying to lead his own band under his own name, Buddy has led the Tommy Dorsey ghost band (a phrase coined by Woody Herman) for many years and continues performing today.

Jimmy Henderson
May 31, 1975 - May 31, 1981

An already famous and popular bandleader who worked in television with all its top stars, Jimmy Henderson was engaged by Glenn Miller Productions in 1975, as the orchestra's new director, opening at the Riverboat in New York. During his reign, the Glenn Miller Orchestra played at President Ronald Reagan's 1981 Inaugural Ball.

Jimmy had done it all. He played both piano and trombone, formed his own dance bands, played in serious orchestras like the Cincinnati Symphony and in the Dr. Simon 100 piece radio concert band performing in concerts, worked night clubs, and played with the big bands of Hal McIntyre, Jimmy and Tommy Dorsey, and for twenty one years he worked as a trombonist in all the major film and television studios.

Jimmy had a respectable six year run as the leader of the Glenn Miller Orchestra that brought the band to new heights of accomplishment. Jimmy retired in 1980 and passed away in New York City in 1998.

In Hollywood, Jimmy Henderson's band was known as "The Entertainment Industry's Own" because he played so many gigs for the Emmy Awards, the Director's Guild of America Awards, and the International Broadcasting Awards.

Larry O'Brien
May 31, 1981 - October 1, 1983

(see page 177)

Dick Gerhart
October 2, 1983 - November 24, 1988

Dick Gerhart and the Glenn Miller Orchestra

LULLABY OF THE RAIN
PIANO SOLO ARRANGEMENT NOW AVAILABLE
Lyric by BARBS FURMAN
Music by LOU RICCA
Introduced and Recorded by
GLENN MILLER
and his Orchestra

The Little Man Who Wasn't There

Lyric by
HAROLD ADAMSON

Music by
BERNARD HANIGHEN

Featured by
GLENN MILLER
and his Orchestra

PART FOUR

THE SONGWRITERS
AND THEIR SONGS

Mack Gordon and Harry Warren
(courtesy 20th Century Fox)

THE SONGWRITERS
AND THEIR SONGS

HARRY WARREN
"CHATTANOOGA CHOO CHOO"

Harry Salvatore Warren is responsible for many first-rate song hits: "Chattanooga Choo Choo," "Jeepers Creepers," "Lullaby of Broadway," the 1942 Oscar nominated song "K-A-L-A-M-A-Z-O-O," "I Found a Million Dollar Baby," "On the Atchison, Topeka and the Santa Fe," "That's Amore," "You're My Everything," "I Had the Craziest Dream," "Boulevard of Broken Dreams," "I Only Have Eyes for You," "At Last," "I Know Why," "You Must Have Been a Beautiful Baby," "Serenade in Blue," "An Affair to Remember," all music composed by Warren with an assortment of collaborators dreaming up the lyrics.

A piano player who, early in his career, performed in a Coney Island, Brooklyn, restaurant and worked his way through songwriter's haven, Tin Pan Alley, Broadway, Radio, and eventually the movies, Harry Warren composed tunes for seventy-five films. Over one-hundred achieved national popularity, many becoming standards.

Harry's main claim to fame is that no other composer could match his record for the 25 year period between 1932 and 1957 in producing music for the movies. He was con-sistently employed by four major film studios. Warren lived to see a revival of interest in his hits of the glory days when, in 1980, *Lullaby of Broadway*, a show with forty-four of his songs, was produced off-Broadway with a small cast.

In August of 1980, famed Broadway producer David Merrick produced a stage version of the 1932 film *Forty-Second Street* for which Warren composed the music. It became one of the greatest box office successes ever held on Broadway, with seventeen Warren songs. It won that year's Antoinette Perry "Tony" award for best musical.

Harry was born in the shadow of the Brooklyn Bridge on Christmas Eve of 1893, the eleventh of twelve children of boot maker Anthony, and his wife, Rachel.

As a kid, he earned money lighting stoves for Jewish families on the Sabbath for the fee of one penny per house. Harry revealed an intense interest in music and sang in the boy's choir of his church. He learned to play an accordion that belonged to his father and continued his interest by playing drums he acquired from a local barber. With a passionate craving for playing music, especially when he attended a concert performed by the famed Boston Symphony, he became transfigured and vowed a life for himself in music.

He learned to play piano, without lessons, and supported himself playing at Vitagraph Film Studios in Brooklyn, New York, playing mood music. He held odd theatrical jobs and earned enough to marry his first love, Josephine Wensler, in December of 1917.

Harry continued to write songs all his life in what turned out be a dream career. *The Laugh Parade*, his first Broadway success, featuring his composition "You're My Everything," became his first major hit. Harry Warren wrote too many songs to document here, but I'm certain they have punctuated many of our own lives at different moments. What was your favorite Harry Warren song?

Mine is "I Had the Craziest Dream," a song my dear friend Helen Forrest performed with Harry James in the film *Springtime in the Rockies*. Helen was at her very best. It was a tough time for her, as she was in love with Harry. Betty Grable ambled along and closed Helen's long affair with Harry James. Helen's biographical book, *I Had the Craziest Dream,* relates her story. Helen was considered the best big band singer of the era.

BING CROSBY, 1975: "For me, Harry Warren occupies a lofty spot among talented and colorful people who wrote great songs which were so important to the advancement of all our careers.

"You know, I thought I had sung all of Harry's big songs, until I looked through the catalogue of his songs, and learned that I missed a lot of them. Harry's brother and official song-plugger, would call on me to record Harry's tunes over the years and he would demonstrate them a cappella, of course—no matter where I happened to be. Backstage, in an alley, at a restaurant, at the racetrack, even at the golf course.

"Harry's film contributions are most impressive. No one has done better. I don't think Harry ever appreciated the immense contribution he had made to popular music, but I do, and I admire and respect him because of it.

"I really think I'd trade anything I've ever done if I could have written just one hit song, and Harry wrote so many. A genuine artist and a warm engaging human being."

MACK GORDON
"CHATTANOOGA CHOO CHOO"

Mack Gordon, the other half of the Harry Warren songwriting team, is certainly an important lyricist for Glenn Miller tunes: "K-A-L-A-M-A-Z-O-O," "Chattanooga Choo Choo," and "At Last." However, Mack Gordon's main collaborator was Harry Ravel, an English born composer. Earlier, he accompanied Mack Gordon on piano when Gordon sang and appeared as a comedian in vaudeville. Gordon's avocation was writing song lyrics. They soon were turning out popular songs together. The two contributed tunes to Broadway's Ziegfeld Follies of 1931. Landing in Hollywood, they signed a Paramount contract, their first effort being "Did You Ever See a Dream Walking" for the 1933 film *Sitting Pretty.* They wound up their collaboration in 1939 after composing "Never in a Million Years," and "There's a Lull in My Life."

At Fox, Mack Gordon worked with Harry Warren on the songs featured in both *Sun Valley Serenade* and *Orchestra Wives.* Besides his great Glenn Miller tunes, Gordon went on to composing lyrics for the songs "You Make Me Feel So Young," a Frank Sinatra standard and "Mam'selle," made popular by vocalist Art Lund.

JOE GARLAND
"In the Mood"

Joe Garland entered into the musical life of Glenn Miller in the most inadvertent way. Glenn and his pianist Chummy MacGregor were entering the Plymouth Hotel in New York City when they were approached by a youngster who was selling music charts for a trumpeter who played in the Louis Armstrong Big Band of 1939. Glenn bought an arrangement of a chart for five dollars, as he sometimes would. Glenn always was interested in obtaining more and more charts because he was always recording and consistently required fresh material.

These sidewalk scores were sold to anyone who had five bucks to spare, so Glenn could not use them in their original state. This particular chart seemed to have possibilities. He was able to utilize the two front saxophone parts and a few parts in the midsection of the piece. Glenn edited it and threw in some solos and worked it up from there. He added to the regular version by including a routine of fading out and returning loudly several times, each time surprising the dancer who thought the tune had ended. MacGregor wrote the finishing coda. On August 1st, 1939, they rehearsed it between sets while performing at the Glen Island Casino, just before they were to play for a radio broadcast. It was played on the air that same night. Yes, the piece was entitled "In the Mood." A well-spent five dollars, you could say!

Joe Garland was an arranger, a composer, a saxophonist, and clarinetist. He studied his craft at Aeolian Conservatory and played in concert bands and orchestras before joining the Seminole Syncopators and also worked for various dance bands. He recorded with legendary pianist Jelly Roll Morton and completed stints with Don Redman and Edgar Hayes before joining Armstrong. His compositions include "Congo Caravan" and "Leap Frog," the latter a popular theme played and recorded by Les Brown's Band of Renown.

Of course, Joe Garland's great claim to fame will always be his composing one of the most popular dance tunes of the Big Band Era, "In the Mood," which helped Glenn Miller establish his phenomenal following. "In the Mood" was originally recorded under the title "There's Rhythm in Harlem" by the Mills Blue Rhythm Band in 1935, and later by the Edgar Hayes Band in early 1938 under the title "In the Mood." But, the composition belongs tightly in the Glenn Miller repertoire.

FIFTEEN "Miller" Songwriters

JOSEPHE WINNER
"Little Brown Jug"

An immensely popular favorite in the Glenn Miller song-book "Little Brown Jug," was written, words and music, by Joseph E. Winner, who used the pseudonym R.A. Eastburn when he composed this catchy little tune in 1869. Yes! 1869. "Little Brown Jug" was popularized by the Weatherwax Brothers Quartet in 1911. It was revised by a Jerry Gray arrangement and ultimately recorded by Glenn in 1939, and remains forever associated with the Glenn Miller Orchestra.

F.W. MEACHAM
"American Patrol"

American Patrol was written in about 1885 by F.W. Meacham and was originally entitled "We Must Be Vigilant." Jerry Gray arranged the march for Glenn in 1942, and it became a tremendous hit.

"String of Pearls"

Jerry Gray, Glenn's ace arranger, composed the music to "String of Pearls" "Pennsylvania 6-5000," and "Sun Valley Jump."

"Tuxedo Junction"

William Johnson, Juliann Dash, Erskine Hawkins and Buddy Feyne collaborated together on the great Miller standard "Tuxedo Junction."

"Sunrise Serenade"

Lyricist Jack Lawrence and piano playing bandleader Frankie Carle, combined their talents composing "Sunrise Serenade," that became Carle's theme and a Glenn Miller staple.

"Elmer's Tune"

"Elmer's Tune," one of Glenn's popular novelty tunes, was written by Sammy Gallup, bandleader Dick Jurgens, and Elmer Albrecht.

"That Old Black Magic"

A popular tune, with a great Miller organization arrangement, was written by the prolific Johnny Mercer, with music by the great Harold Arlen of *Wizard of Oz* songs fame. It became the theme song of night club icon Billy Daniels. Of course, Arlen wrote many standards: "Blues in the Night," "Come Rain or Come Shine," and "It's Only a Paper Moon." Mercer lyricised "My Shining Hour," "Fools Rush In," "Satin Doll," and "Jeepers Creepers." And many more. Mercer also contributed to "Skylark," with music by Hoagy Carmichael of "Stardust" fame.

"Don't Sit Under the Apple Tree" {with Anyone Else but Me}

This 1942 hit for Glenn was written by Sammy Stept ("Time Waits for No One"), Charles Tobias, ("Please Don't Talk About Me When I'm Gone" and ("At Last") and Lew Brown ("Life is Just a Bowl of Cherries"). It was based on an old 1833 tune called "Long Long Ago." The Andrews Sisters performed the song in the film *Private Buckaroo*, appearing with comedian Joe E. Lewis.

"Perfidia"

"Perfidia" was written for Gene Autry in the Western film, *Stardust on the Sage* in 1941 by Milton Leeds and Alberto Dominquez. Glenn's treatment is absolutely the better of all versions.

"Moonlight Cocktail"

Another film claims "Moonlight Cocktail." This time it's a Marx Brothers vehicle called *A Night in Casablanca*, released in 1942, with words and music by Kim Gannon (of "You Are Always in My Heart" and "I'll Be Home or Christmas" fame) and C. Luckeyth Roberts. The film was also based on Roberts composition "Ripples of the Nile."

"St. Louis Blues March"

The "St. Louis Blues" was composed by legendary W.C. Handy and performed by Bing Crosby in *The Birth of the Blues*. Ray McKinley revised the old blues rendition at Yale University, on the New Haven Green, during the war when Glenn first organized the Army Air Force Band, instilling a little swing into the marching music with Jerry Gray writing up a full band arrangement and converting the blues tune into one of the most famous Glenn Miller arrangements of any composition.

"A Nightingale Sang in Berkeley Square"

This tune was composed by Eric Maschwitz, Manning Sherwin, and Jack Strachey in 1940. This is one of Glenn's and Ray Eberle's best efforts, although England's premier singer Dame Vera Lynn recorded a perfect version, as did jazz vocalist Anita O'Day.

"Indian Summer"

This evergreen was composed by Victor Herbert in 1919 and revised by Glenn in 1940 when famed lyricist Al Dubin added the words. Ray Eberle excels on the recording of this beautiful and charming melody. Victor Herbert wrote an endless list of songs that includes "Gypsy Love Song," and "I'm Falling in Love with Someone," from his operettas.

"Pavanne"

This Morton Gould composition was written in 1938 for his "American Symphonette No. 2."

"Danny Boy"

"Danny Boy" is a conversion of a 1913 composition by Frederick Edward Weatherly and is based on the Irish traditional "Londonderry Air" of 1855. Larry O'Brien performs this beautiful tune perfectly on his trombone. Larry once played it just for my wife Madeline and I during a rehearsal at Westhampton Beach Performing Arts Center in July of 2003. Wow!

Sun Valley Serenade
1941

Chattanooga Choo Choo

Dorothy Dandridge and the Nicholas Brothers

(courtesy 20th Century Fox)

MOVIE PORTRAITS
SUN VALLEY SERENADE

20th Century Fox

Starring internationally famous skating champion, Sonja Henie, with John Payne, Milton Berle, Lynn Bari, Joan Davis, vocalist/dancer Dorothy Dandridge, and featured the excellent dancing of the Nicholas Brothers.

Synopsis: In this lightheartred comedy of romance and music, the Glenn Miller Orchestra accompanies John Payne, Sonja Henie and comedian Milton Berle through a typical Hollywood film of the forties. Glenn leads a struggling band named the Dartmouth Troubadours that is about to get their big break at the posh Sun Valley ski resort. The romance between singer Vivian Dawn, actually actress Lynn Bari, and piano player Ted Scott, (John Payne) is damaged by a publicity stunt set up by band manager "Nifty" Allen (Milton Berle). He had arranged for Ted to adopt a war refugee, making him become responsible for a beautiful Norwegian ice skater who decides she wants to marry him. The rest of the story is fun-filled with Glenn's great music and fancy figure skating by Henie.

SONGS: "It Happened in Sun Valley," "I Know Why," "The Kiss Polka," "Chattanooga Choo Choo," all songs by Harry Warren and Mack Gordon.

Comments from Metronome Magazine music critic Barry Ulanov:

"Never has a movie made more of a popular band, and never has a movie featuring such an organization presented its music so tastefully. From the shadowed figures of the bandsmen which serve as a background to the credit titles of the picture to the easy presentation of the rehearsal scene that features 'Chattanooga Choo Choo,' the band is really brilliantly directed, lighted, photographed.

"It's a wonderful film showcasing the Glenn Miller Orchestra. After a few bars of their theme, 'Moonlight Serenade,' with a happily grinning Miller directing, and the audiences in the film houses going mad as they recognize the band and the music, the boys go into a pleasant tune that features Lynn Bari singing. Though the band has never played with Lynn before, they back her with smooth perfection and the Modernaires harmonize with her without a hitch.

"Pictorially, Trigger Alpert and Maurice Purtill take the honors. Trigger hops around like mad, and Maurice looks like the movies idea of a swing drummer, all right.

They stay within the bounds of good taste, however, and the rest of the band just looks happy, and, as if they play for a living rather than chew scenery. The story is believable, and happily centers around the band, so that the whole thing is a triumph for Glenn Miller and the band."

Glenn approached the making and participation in this, their first film, as a stickler for the truth about a band and how it really operated, insisting the script be believable, before he would sign his contract. He insisted the band be integrated into the story line, and not just showcased in some unimportant scene the way the Dorsey's did in *Las Vegas Nights*, Artie Shaw did in the film *Dancing Co-Ed*, and Benny Goodman with *Hollywood Hotel*.

Glenn was totally satisfied with the treatment in the film of his biggest hit "Chattanooga Choo Choo," performed by vocalist Dorothy Dandridge and the wonderful, dancing Nicholas Brothers. For many film goers, this may have been the best treatment of a Glenn Miller hit they would remember all their lives. The songs were composed by Harry Warren and lyricist Mack Gordon, who went on to write the songs for the subsequent Glenn Miller film, *Orchestra Wives*.

(courtesy 20th Century Fox)

Harry James, Mack Gordon, Glenn, Harry Warren and Sammy Kaye

(courtesy 20th Century Fox)

ORCHESTRA WIVES

20th Century Fox - 1942

Starring George Montgomery, Lynn Bari, Cesar Romero, Jackie Gleason, Ann Rutherford, Mary Beth Hughes, Virginia Gilmore, Carole Landis, Glenn Miller, Tex Beneke and the Orchestra, and vocalist Marion Hutton.

Synopsis: A new bride of one of Glenn's musicians finds the strain of a musicians life on the road too much. Leader Gene Morrison (Glenn) sets out on a national tour with the band, when trumpeter Bill Abbott (George Montgomery), Impulsively marries an ardent fan named Connie (Ann Rutherford), who at first is willing to endure the rigor of spending her life without the presence of her husband. Through gossip of the other orchestra wives, she thinks her husband is involved with an old flame. The ensuing belief threatens to end the band and marriage.

Orchestra Wives, a follow-up of the successful film *Sun Valley Serenade*, was conceived to showcase, once again, the very popular Glenn Miller Orchestra in a story that sheds some light into the lives of big band musicians who were on constant tour during the height of the Big Band Era, and to present a batch of very worthy, irresistible Harry Warren tunes that have lived on within the charts of the world famous Glenn Miller Orchestra for more than 60 years. The film enveloped a similar plot like *Sun Valley Serenade* with musical interludes. All five Harry Warren and Mack Gordon songs, written expressly for the movie, were recorded by Glenn. "That's Sabotage," "People Like You and Me," which were World War II songs, and the famed "Kalamazoo," "At Last," and most stirring, "Serenade in Blue," were all successful numbers.

The love ballad, "At Last" was subsequently recorded by Glenn with Ray Eberle on the vocal. "Kalamazoo" became extremely popular with Tex Beneke singing the K-A-L-A-M-A-Z-O-O staccato voicing. Harry Warren said that he first wrote the complete melody of "Kalamazoo" as a rhythmic exercise, with no thought of attaching lyrics, but Mack Gordon came up with the novel idea for the words of the song. Fitting those words to the music was considered a very neat and clever piece of lyric writing.

The ballad "Serenade in Blue," with the memorable introduction by arranger Billy May, has become a standard. It is a superior piece of music that allows for all manner of harmonizing.

> *Harry Warren: "I credit Glenn Miller as the source of my inspiration. In writing songs for movies I had always cut my cloth to the performer and this was often a limiting factor. But I knew that Glenn could play anything I put on paper and that he would arrange the music in a way that could only enhance it. I liked him very much."*

According to Harry Warren, Glenn was a gentle, quiet man who never raised his voice, and whom he considered a fine musician. Warren thought it ridiculous that some referred to Glenn as a wartime Lawrence Welk. Warren was sure that Glenn's work was the most important influence of the Big Band Era.

As his take for *Orchestra Wives*, Glenn earned over $100,000.00, and used $ 75,000.00 of it to buy a 55 acre fruit farm in Monrovia, California, which he called *Tuxedo Junction*, named after his successful recording by the same name.

THE GLENN MILLER STORY

Universal Studios, 1954

Hollywood Version of the Biography of Glenn Miller
   Produced by Aaron Rosenberg and directed by Anthony Mann, it stars James Stewart as Glenn Miller, and June Allyson as Helen Miller, Charles Drake as Glenn's manager and friend Don Haynes, Harry Morgan, as piano player Chummy MacGregor, with appearances by Louis Armstrong, Frances Langford, Gene Krupa, Ben Pollack, and featuring the Modernaires.

JUNE ALLYSON

When James Stewart and June Allyson appeared in the The Glenn Miller Story, both had to tour internationally as part of the deal to promote the film.

"The interest in the film was amazing," said June, "we toured Europe, Germany, Italy, France, and London, which I loved, and also in Spain and even Holland. Everyone was really interested. That's because music is the international language. It was the

Paul Tanner and June Allyson
(John Tumpak photo)

story of a man and his music. No one danced, and nobody sang, except in one number with Frances Langford and the Modernaires"

The Glenn Miller story was admittedly one of the highlights of June Allyson's long career. She had performed in many MGM musicals including Good News, in which she sang and danced, "The Varsity Drag" with Peter Lawford, and "Good News" with a very young Mel Tormé. She also performed in *Two Girls and a Sailor, Best Foot Forward*, and the remake of *Broadway Melody.*

"I know this sounds like it's not true, but it is. I would go onto the set when I didn't have to be there just to hear the wonderful music. And those musicians, well, you knew the music would never die. And to watch Jimmy (Stewart) learn to play the trombone, it was such hard work for him. His sound was actually very bad, but he had to position the slide in the right place for the camera. Joe Yuki actually recorded it. They finally plugged up the horn, but all his moves turned out right. He worked on it for months. Honest, Glenn's music will be with us forever, long after we are gone." June played the part of Glenn's wife, Helen Miller. For June, the film was also about the life of Helen Miller, who showed up every day at the movie set.

"Helen was an ordinary and very bright young girl who came from Iowa, just like Glenn. He was in and out of her life, at school and afterwards. She never thought they would finally marry until one day he calls her and tells her, 'You've gotta come and marry me.' And, she did! As the story shows you, she was his backbone. He had one thing in his head, and that was to establish his 'sound.' When he found it, he gave her credit too. She made him work to find it. They adored each other. I loved making that film for those reasons alone." June Allyson lives in California among many of her friends.

JAMES STEWART

According to band trombonist, Paul Tanner, who was a consultant for *The Glenn Miller Story* and the only actual band alumnus to appear on the screen, he admired Jimmy Stewart's effort at learning how to manipulate the trombone to make it appear as if Glenn was actually playing the instrument:

"He learned the slide positions of every single note he was supposed to play, even though Dick Nash, Joe Yuki, or

I did the actual playing in the movie. He'd also stuff up the mouthpiece to get the inflated cheek effect. He was incredibly conscientious. We became friends on a need-to-know basis, and he kept watching me like a hawk. He was an awfully quick learner."

Pianist Chummy MacGregor was a consultant to the film. Henry Morgan, later a star of the television show M*A*S*H, portrayed Chummy in the film. Universal gave the movie all the backing it needed, and their choice of James Stewart as Glenn, enabled it to became one of Jimmy's best successes. He was an excellent choice and even resembled Glenn in bearing and scholarly appearance. His previous training in music helped him simulate playing the trombone.

> *Jimmy Stewart: "I was impressed with the presentation of 'Moonlight Serenade.' I was at the piano. I'd hit a note, write it down, hit another. In the background, so faint at first you could hardly hear it, were the chords. Then I'd write, then you'd hear the beat, and then we slowly fade into an enormous dance hall, where the whole orchestra is playing 'Moonlight Serenade', the first song, as far as I know, that really had the Glenn Miller sound."*

Many critics and fans considered the movie to be stuffed with over sentimentality and banality, although it turned out to be an enormous success and Hollywood's third largest money earner of the year 1954, behind *White Christmas*, with Bing Crosby and Danny Kaye, and *The Caine Mutiny* with Humphrey Bogart.

The movie ranks high in following the facts of Glenn's life with exception of the event where Glenn discovers his "sound."

For me, the *Glenn Miller Story* was a valid vehicle showcasing Glenn's music, re-establishing tremendous interest in his celebrated recordings, introducing his timeless music to an entirely new generation. Sure, it was partially a Hollywood fantasy film, but it absolutely glorified Glenn and his music. No one was harmed by this, and according to many others, it brought Glenn's music back into focus and impressed many budding musicians here and abroad who, inspired, translated their musical influences over to Glenn's material. Its far-reaching effects on countless musicians worldwide has insured Glenn's music will be carried forward beyond the 21st Century.

PART FIVE

THE GLENN MILLER ORCHESTRAS OVER THERE

Ray McVay and the Glenn Miller Orchestra in England

Glenn's Brother
Herb Miller
and Roy Belcher

Herb Miller with Roy Belcher - 1983
(Roy Belcher collection)

ROY BELCHER SPEAKS

Richard Grudens: *"Ever since I began writing about the Big Bands and their participants covering what we all call the Big Band Era, Roy Belcher, as President of Big Bands International, has been an inspiration and a friend, a person who has championed and worked hard for the proliferation of the greatest popular music ever."*

"I am delighted to write here about the biggest name by far in the world of Big Bands—Glenn Miller. As an Englishman I had seen Glenn Miller on film and heard the band on recordings played on radio or at home and had marveled at the quality of his music.

"Then, on June 28, 1944, Captain Glenn Miller brought his AEF Orchestra to Britain, and shortly after at the Annual Jazz Jamboree in London. I eventually saw the orchestra, one of over a dozen bands at this great festival, and all in one day and on the same stage. Miller, as a front man, was serious and to the point in his announcements at the microphone, and maintained a formal attitude to the orchestra at all times. The orchestra made broadcasts from the Corn Exchange in Bedford—nicknamed by Glenn and the band as *Lombardo Hall* after Guy Lombardo. Among the guest vocalists were Bruce Trent, Anne Shelton and Dorothy Carless.

"One of the most memorable concerts the orchestra performed was in July, 1944 at Wycombe Abbey, the Headquarters of General Jimmy Doolittle, in High Wycombe, Buckinghamshire. The band played on a flatbed truck trailer in front of the Abbey and the General attended along with thousands of servicemen.

"Johnny Desmond and the Crew Chiefs handled the vocals including such favorites as 'Moonlight Serenade,' 'Stardust,' and 'I'll Get By.' The following day Miller and Don Haynes toured Mole's Hole, the nearby underground military establishment serving the Allies in the European Centre of Operations, all which still exists.

Roy Belcher in his office

"During his time in Britain, playing to service audiences all over the UK and making numerous broadcasts, the influence of Glenn Miller's AEF Orchestra on British musicians and bands became increasingly noticeable. Bands here had previously been relatively unadventurous in arrangements and instrumentation. Soloists were now inspired to play loud licks, and swing numbers became more frequently heard in programs that had previously been predominantly vocal dance tunes, and ensemble sizes increased to contain eight brass and five reeds.

"Glenn left for Paris in what was to be a fatal flight from Twinwood Farm, a small RAF Aerodrome that has, in recent times, been made into a Glenn Miller tourist attraction by Twinwood Events.

"It is recorded by the WAAF Corporal duty radio operator, at Twinwood at the time, that within just a few minutes of his takeoff, radio contact with Miller was lost. This had led to the interesting conjecture that his plane may have crashed on the English mainland and become buried in the ground. There are, of course, numerous other 'explanations' of his disappearance, these generally made by writers with a financial interest in propounding their own proposal, and some of them highly improbable.

"In 1981, Glenn's younger brother, Herb, came to England, and after playing with local bands, decided to form his own big band. "This was a full-sized, sixteen piece band playing the music of Glenn Miller. Herb called his orchestra 'Herb Miller's Sixteen Great Britons.' Over the course of some years they attained a peak when they reproduced the Glenn Miller sound as well as any British band had previously done. Bookings became good for the Herb Miller Orchestra from around 1983, when the band played the inaugural Big Band weekend at Pontin's Pakefield Central in Suffolk, a place eventually to become known as 'The home of the Big Bands in Europe.'

"The Herb Miller Orchestra played two special concerts with full string section at Wycombe Abbey in Buckinghamshire—recreating Glenn's AEF Orchestra's open-air concert, [held on a flat bed trailer with buzz bombs flying overhead] at this very same spot during WW2 and, which was featured in the film *The Glenn Miller Story.* Former Miller clarinet player, and later leader, Peanuts Hucko, was a special guest at one of these concerts, as were many British personalities with Miller associations.

"But, since 1988, Britain has had its own Glenn Miller Orchestra UK. Originally created by Ray McVay and John Watson by arrangement with Glenn Miller Productions, and now for some years directed solely by McVay, successfully touring the UK and occasional overseas tours including Japan and South America. The Glenn Miller Orchestra UK has become famed for their faithful recreation of original Miller Numbers and has access to the original Miller charts. The band benefits from being almost fully acoustic—an uncommon feature in the UK.

"For many years London has been the home of an active Glenn Miller Society. Meetings are held with recitals and talks. Co-founder Geoffrey E. Butcher, the noted big band historian who wrote *Next to a Letter from Home - Major Glenn Miller's Wartime Band* published in 1986. The title derived from Lt. General James H. Doolittle's statement in July 1944: 'Next to a letter from home, Major Miller, your organization is the greatest morale booster in the European Theater.' The book deals with the disappearance mystery of Major Miller and contains a day-by-day chronology of the orchestra from June 28, 1944 to July 28, 1945. Butcher also penned the serialized The Ted Heath Band Story in Big Bands International Magazine.

"In 1967, Syd Lawrence launched his orchestra in England, with its style majoring on Glenn Miller music. This orchestra has been very popular over the years and achieved that Glenn Miller sound by virtue of Lawrence's skillful arrangements and continues today touring the UK. It has been voted the Favourite Band in the UK by BBI members in Big Bands International Magazine.

"Big Bands International (BBI), which I launched in 1977 as a magazine to cover all the big bands, was my hobby activity, but swiftly became a near full time occupation. BBI has carried out a Members Favourite Band Poll for many years, entered separately for the UK and USA. The band with the most votes overall throughout is Glenn Miller. The magazine is ongoing, and has established a website: www.bigbandsinternational.org. During the years I published the magazine, the most frequent letters received from members and fans was regarding Glenn Miller.

"Considering the Miller band was formed pre-WW II, the fact that it remains so popular after some 65 years is a tribute to the quality of the music and the creativeness of its leader. Glenn made memorable music and I am confident that in another 65 years Glenn Miller's music will still be popular and will be prominent in everyone's music history books."

Roy Belcher, Founder Big Bands International, London, England, October 2003.

The Glenn Miller Orchestra
"Over There"
with Max Wirz

Max with Andy Prior

with Ray McVay

with Hazy Osterwald

Wil Salden

GLENN MILLER'S MUSIC "OVER THERE!"

To add to the scope of this wondrous Glenn Miller Orchestra story, we enlisted our dear friend, Swiss Big Band and Dixieland music host for Radio Eviva, Max Wirz, to comb through Glenn's European counterparts, old and new, and bring to us their own Glenn Miller story. Max is Switzerland's legendary radio host who contributed to our Big Band book, "Jukebox Saturday Night" in 1999, presenting his account of the Big Band scene in Europe and England. This time he met with and interviewed Europe and England's current and official Glenn Miller Orchestra leaders, Europe's Will Salden and England's Ray McVay.

Max filed his first installment after sitting down with Wil Salden and his business partner, Jutta Schmidt, immediately following a one night stand for Wil's big Glenn Miller Orchestra at the Tonhalle in St. Gallen, located in Eastern Switzerland. Wil Salden leads Continental Europe's only licensed Glenn Miller Orchestra.

In late September, 2003, Max interviewed Britain's Ray McVay aboard the Queen Elizabeth II as it crossed the Atlantic with Ray performing Glenn Miller music aboard the great cruise ship. Max caught up with Ray in New York, the day following a "Glenn" book meeting with Max, his wife Nelly, and me, and my wife Madeline, at the famed Three Village Inn, where we meet annually.

Max Wirz is the quintessential fan of the big bands and has established lasting friendships with many of the notable bandleaders and their sidemen from Europe and England. Aside from his interviews with Glenn Miller leaders Wil Salden and Ray McVay, he talked Glenn Miller music with Billy Gorlt, Andy Prior, John Miller (Herb Miller's son and Glenn's nephew) Peanuts Hucko, Thilo Wolf, Oski Brunnschwiler, Pepe Lienhard, Paul Kuhn, Dani Felber, Hugo Strasser, Hazy Osterwald, Bryan Pendleton, Wiebe Schuurmans, and Freddy Staff. That's quite an impressive list of great musicians.

Read on about the Glenn Miller overseas spirit, a spirit that defies time and language, a spirit located deep within each of these great musicians musical hearts, a spirit that has inspired each of them to continue the tradition that Glenn originated and that has lasted all these years.

· · · · ·

BBI FAVOURITE BANDS

ANNUAL POLL 2002 RESULTS

UK:

PRESENT:
1   SYD LAWRENCE
2   TED HEATH
3   GLENN MILLER
4   BBC BIG BAND

PAST:
1   TED HEATH
2   GLENN MILLER
3   COUNT BASIE
4   STAN KENTON

USA:

PRESENT:
1   MAYNARD FERGUSON
2   WOODY HERMAN
3   GLENN MILLER
4   STAN KENTON

PAST:
1   STAN KENTON
2   GLENN MILLER
3   WOODY HERMAN
4   COUNT BASIE

JOHN MILLER

HERB MILLER'S SON, NEPHEW TO GLENN

> *"You'll find everything in Glenn Miller's music that you find in Bach, Beethoven, Ravel and Strauss."*
> —John Miller 2003

At Pontin's Holiday Center in Pakefield, on the windblown Eastern coast of England, Max Wirz converses with John Miller as he explains about his connection to Glenn Miller:

"There were three brothers, and a sister: Deane, Glenn, with two n's, my father, Herb, and Irene, all gone now. I am Herb Miller's son, making me Glenn Miller's nephew. The Herb Miller Orchestra was formed by my father twenty-three years ago, in 1980. He ran it until 1987, when he passed on to someplace better, I hope. Rather than see the orchestra fall, I took over and have been running things since. After fifteen years, everyone thought it was time the name be changed, and so it was then billed as John Miller and his Orchestra."

Originally, John's father worked in the states and when he was asked to come to England to form a big band, he agreed, taking John along. By 1995, the band performed about 130 dates per year. In 1995 the band toured with Peanuts Hucko, of the original band, along with his wife, the former Mrs. Harry James, vocalist Louise Tobin. Peanuts earlier fronted the Glenn Miller Orchestra in the United States from January through September of 1974.

Max brought up the subject to John about the validity of the movie *The Glenn Miller Story,* always a contention among original participants and fans.

"There were a lot of true things in the movie and, of course, a lot of Hollywood items that were not accurate. One true thing: Helen would always say, 'Oh, Glenn! Honestly!' It was her favorite saying, and June Allyson repeated that often in the film. However, Glenn was a very positive guy, nothing like the Jimmy Stewart personality. Stewart handled the slide on the trombone very faithfully, close to what he would have to do, had he been actually playing. Paul Tanner coached him.

Herb Miller
(R. Grudens collection)

"Glenn knew exactly what he was doing. He did call Helen after a year and said, 'Come to New York, I am going to marry you. 'Not, what do you think?, or should we? When Helen said that she was engaged to the son of the hardware store owner, a very lucrative family with money, Glenn simply said: 'Have him drive you to the station!' And, he did. Glenn knew exactly what he was doing. He didn't know how to lose."

Currently, John Miller is doing everything connected with music. A friend, popular bandleader Andy Prior, showcased in the book by Richard Grudens, *Jukebox Saturday Night*, have been performing together on special events. The full sized band is still touring England performing basically Glenn Miller, because, as John says: "It's Miller, because I am a Miller."

Although John is an accomplished trombone player, he readily leaves the playing to those in the band he feels are better. Unlike the 130 shows per year accomplished in 1995, the band now performs about 75 shows per year with the John Miller Orchestra.

For John Miller, the Miller name evokes magic among fans attending shows, but the name doesn't work, unless, as John says, "No matter whose nephew you are, it means little unless you deliver, and give them something of your own. Just being a nephew is not enough. Gathering good musicians to play is very important for the band. John is a good front man, much like his uncle Glenn once was, and the players say he is tops with them.

Max brought up the question of the Glenn Miller Centenary, celebrating the 100th birthday of Glenn Miller and the 60th Anniversary of his disappearance.

"Well, Max, we have already made plans. The Miller Family Birthday Party is already booked at various venues all over England. Besides Wynne Miller, Glenn's niece, whose dad was my uncle, Deane Miller, I remain the last blood relative active in show business. It's not surprising that Glenn's music is still popular today. It was designed for people. It is good solid music. You'll find everything in Miller music that you find in Bach, Beethovan, Ravel, and Strauss. It's happy music and it should appeal today as it did sixty years ago. I think it will never be forgotten," to which Max fully agreed.

WIL SALDEN AND THE WORLD - FAMOUS GLENN MILLER ORCHESTRA OF EUROPE

> *"For arrangements, we needed the real thing. So we became an official Glenn Miller Orchestra with his original charts."*
> —Wil Salden

Continental Europe's only licensed Glenn Miller Orchestra came through Switzerland for a one night stand at the Tonhalle in St. Gallen which is located in Eastern Switzerland. Our own Max Wirz was there, taking the opportunity to visit with Wil and business manager Jutta Schmidt to learn more about the Glenn Miller European connection.

Wil Salden was born after the end of the Big Band Era, on June 14, 1950, and was educated in Holland, majoring in piano. He led his own small bands, and played for the Hilversum Radio and TV Orchestra to become its director. Eventually becoming a stellar musician, Wil found his way into Glenn Miller's great music.

Wil: "At a young stage in my life, I was fully and completely attracted by Swing Era music, which was also played by other great bands of the era. The Glenn Miller sound does not distinguish itself through trombones, or brass instruments from other bands. Of course, it is true that Glenn Miller created that famous Miller sound by adding a clarinet to the saxophones, and that he used trumpets and trombones as leading elements in his music. The fact that he played trombone, was of no particular interest to me. He might as well have played trumpet. It was the swing in his music that attracted me. Furthermore, he played commercial music. It was simple with straight forward melodies that the listeners

Wil Salden and his Orchestra

and dancers could follow and understand. Today, the kids would call this ingenious."

Wil Salden formed his big band in 1985 and began touring Europe as The Glenn Miller Revival Orchestra. Their first concert was in Hof-Saale, in central Germany. Only days before Wil was rebuilding the brass and saxophone sections, and one hour before the curtain rose, he remained busy with notating finishing touches on some arrangements. The band played a selection of big band popular selections, but Wil found himself leaning towards favoring the music of Glenn Miller.

"But, the question was, how do I get the original Miller arrangements? We worked from transcriptions, but we needed the real thing. It did not make sense to me to try to outdo Glenn Miller, because he had some of the best arrangers of the time working for his band.

"From reading about Glenn and listening to musicians who knew and worked with him, I got the feeling that he understood what the public wanted and was able to deliver it. And, he led the band with a firm hand, which I try to emulate. It is in the nature of musicians to interpret and improvise, but Glenn would not have any of this. I am convinced that the success and following we enjoy is due to sticking to the original arrangements. Don't misunderstand me, however, while we discipline ourselves, we don't play the music to death."

The first appearance of Wil Salden's Glenn Miller Revival Orchestra was a big success. Reviews were good, causing bookings to come in from professional and private organizers throughout the country. In early 1990, with Wil still searching for those elusive arrangements, he received an invitation from Glenn Miller Productions to obtain a license. On March 16, 1990, at a ceremony in New York, David Mackay, Jr., President of Glenn Miller Productions, presented Wil Salden with that license which allowed him to lead an exclusive Glenn Miller Orchestra throughout Europe. It included the countries of Belgium, Netherlands, Luxembourg, Germany, Austria, France, Italy, Denmark, Sweden, Norway, Finland, Czech Republic, Slovakia, Poland, Hungary and Switzerland, the later made our correspondent Max Wirz extremely happy.

Wil Salden, Wiebe Schuuremans and Jutta Schmidt
(courtesy Max Wirz)

"Seventeen years after that first successful concert in Hof-Saale, and during many concerts that followed, I have noticed the audiences have changed. They are becoming younger. When a particular song is performed, or when a musician delivers an unusual solo, they show appreciation in a manner their parents did not. They whistle and stomp their feet. Remember, the crowds back then were of the elder generation. Our fans have grown older with us. Astoundingly, they have been bringing younger fans with them, so the people are mixed with three generations in the audience."

With rare individuals around who personally witnessed the music of Glenn Miller, there otherwise remains enough around who remember the short wave BBC radio programs that broadcast the American Band of the Allied Expeditionery Force Orchestra music conducted by Glenn Miller himself. Today, besides Glenn's music, pieces by Ray Anthony and Billy May, both alumnus of the original, civilian Glenn Miller Orchestra, are also featured by Wil Salden. They try to play many signature pieces of the great bandleaders. In 2003, to commemorate Bing Crosby's birth in 1903, and in memory of Bing's long time singing partner, Rosemary Clooney, Wil's own singer, Mariske Hekkenberg, and Wil, performed a duet of "On a Slow Boat to China" from an arrangement by Billy May. Wil's trombone players get a chance to play solos with Tommy Dorsey's songs. Interestingly, Glenn's arrangements contain no trombone solos, but frequently and strongly feature the entire trombone section. Wil Salden does not write his own arrangements. He leaves that to the musicians and arrangers in his organization.

Schmidt and Salden, composed of Wil Salden and Jutta Schmidt, own and manage the organization in their principal office, Hammersbach, near Frankfurt on Main, Germany.

"It's right, Max. I am the business manager and Wil is the music man. My job is to handle the commercial aspects, as well as the office and band personnel. We perform roughly 200 concerts annually, mostly one night stands. That covers about 190 cities in the European countries. We cover an area that reaches from Lahti, just to the North of Helsinki, Finland, to Messina, Sicily, and from Den Haag in Holland to Warsaw, Poland."

The office in Hammersbach does the routing and planning for the orchestra. Nine lady employees run things, with half working mornings, and the other half the afternoon. They schedule the bus, and make hotel reservations, and keep the bus stocked with merchandise, such as program books and CDs. Jutta Schmidt travels with the orchestra whenever possible. Remaining close with promoters and audiences allows Jutta to track fans wishes, and permits her to implement adaptations as necessary. Like Glenn Miller, she too runs a tight ship, a probable reason for their success.

Wil simply loves to make music. Being professional and successful guarantees continuous bookings for the band. With double coverage on all instruments, the musicians, mostly the younger ones, like to do stints with other bands where they can experiment with other musical styles. The musicians enjoy that, so they tend to remain with the band for longer periods. In any one year no more than a few players permanently leave the band.

Wil: "Our musicians are mainly from Germany and Holland, and even from Switzerland, Max. In fact, for trumpet and trombone sections, we can call upon local musicians. For instance, if we need a trumpet and flugelhorn in Switzerland, we call on Dani Felber, who leads his own band. Around Berlin we have several musicians who work for the RIAS Big Band, who are available on short notice. In this respect, we are luckier than band leaders in America, where the distances between gigs are further apart. With respect to the age of our musicians, Wiebe Schuurmans, one of our saxophone players, and a singer in the Moonlight Serenaders, is seventy-four. He has been with me since the beginning. The youngest, Herwin Lokken, is a twenty-four year old trumpet player."

For the Glenn Miller centenary, Wil and Jutta are in touch with radio stations, suggesting they play an abundance of Glenn Miller music. The same applies to television stations, suggesting they feature Glenn Miller films, and musical arrangements of Glenn's in variety shows."

Jutta Schmidt: " Although most radio and TV orchestras have been disbanded, the former band leaders, Paul Kuhn, Hugo Strasser, Max Greger, Peter Herbholzheimer, are perfectly able to produce the unique and special Glenn Miller sound, and so would Thilo Wolf, who features "Swing It," a special on Bavarian television every two years. We are also thinking of taking with us on the tours, an exhibition of The Glenn Miller Story, consisting of memorabilia and photos. And, in honor of Glenn Miller, it is our declared ambition to perform at least two hundred concerts during 2004. For Wil Salden and Jutta Schmidt, the year 2004 will be an even more memorable experience for the world famous Glenn Miller Orchestra under Wil Salden's excellent direction.

Wil Salden's Moonlight Serenaders
L-R: Wil, Uli Plettendorf, Miet Molnar and Erik Hilferink

RAY McVAY

England's Own Glenn Miller Orchestra Leader

> *"Moonlight Serenade"* always receives the strongest and longest applause.
>
> —Ray McVay

Sitting with Ray McVay in state room 2085, Max chatted with him about his unique musical ties to Glenn Miller:

"When I was about twelve, my dad would take me to the local record store on Saturday's where it was a tradition that he would buy at least one new record. My dad and brother were musicians. We looked at all the new records that had come in, like Benny Goodman, Harry James, and Glenn Miller. When I heard Harry James' 'Trumpet Blues' I thought that it was absolutely brilliant, gorgeous. Well, we listened to all the great bands then. Along the way I heard Glenn Miller's 'In the Mood.' I thought that was also fantastic. Then, dad played something softer, 'Moonlight Serenade.' Oh! My God! That was great and it sort of got me switched on to Glenn Miller.

As time progressed I received music lessons on the clarinet and saxophone. By the time I was 18, I began playing in different semipro local bands. My dad helped placed me in other bands, as well, so I could get as much experience as possible.

Max detected Ray's voice as sounding a bit Scottish.

"Yes, Max, you are right. That was in Gourock, Scotland, an hour drive from Glasgow, where Glenn Miller and his Orchestra and a lot of American troops came in during World War II. You see, I was attached to Glenn Miller from the very beginning. By eighteen I got tired busking with local bands, where you could not make any money. I told my dad I was going to London to

THE GLENN MILLER ORCHESTRA (UK) *directed by* **RAY McVAY**

try my luck. He was apprehensive, but blessed me going. "In London, I played with various groups and wound up in a rock and roll band, becoming musical director with Larry Parnes, who imported American singers, but not necessarily their musicians. Our one group would be used to back them all. We played for Little Richard, Tom Jones, Engelbert - and it was fun as we all were so young.

"But, I had to get back to the big bands and Miller-type music. I auditioned for an organization in England called Mecca Dancing. Every big city had a Mecca Ballroom where everybody was dancing at that time. Later, they hired us to play at the Lyceum Ballroom on the Strand in London. This was my big challenge. I worked there for three and a half years and then over to the Hammersmith Palais, a really famous dancer's ballroom, and remained for four years. During the Lyceum tenure, we worked on a BBC television show, Come Dancing, doing twelve shows annually for twelve years running. It involved Glenn Miller style material in waltzes, fox trots, quicksteps, all of them. For me, playing Glenn Miller was great, as I loved his stuff and the public loved it, as well.

After twelve years, Ray McVay became restless, anxious to return to touring with his band. He hired an agent, and with a name recognition, played in many different venues performing on one night stands and enjoying it. This, when the bands of Syd Lawrence, Joe Loss, and Ted Heath were also touring.

For Ray McVay, the music of Glenn Miller was always close to his heart. He wanted to do a tribute to Glenn, even though it had been done by Lawrence and others. Ray wanted to bring in former Miller musicians, like Willie Schwartz, Billy May, Zeke Zarchy and Jimmy Priddy. But, Willie was too busy, as was May, in their own ventures.

"In the Spring of 1986, however, Willie, Jimmy and Zeke came over and joined our tour. When we did 'Moonlight Serenade' with Willie on clarinet, you could hear a pin drop. It was absolutely immaculate. When the orchestra finished playing the audience stood up, applauded and applauded."

On a day off, Ray, as a surprise, arranged for the former Miller trio to enjoy a day of golf at St. Andrew's famous golf course. They were all golfers, and had told Ray about golf anecdotes with Glenn, about the time when Glenn could not sleep and called the guys at six AM, after only four hours sleep, saying, "Let's play golf!"

"I picked them up saying we would take a ride into the countryside. They were happy, but when we came over a hill and they saw St. Andrews Golf Course sign, you should have seen their faces. And they were totally surprised when they learned I had arranged for them to play the old, sacred links."

After the game the three bought up all the souvenirs they could carry to take back to their friends in the States. Willie Schwartz said: "I will never forget this as long as I live." That was Ray McVay's true introduction to Glenn Miller, working and playing with three Miller musicians, and friends.

To add to the current success of the band after the Royal Festival Hall concert, two Japanese businessmen requested Ray's card, declaring the concert marvelous, and within a few months were invited to tour Japan, performing one tour a year for four years. "We were a success in Japan and did the tour four times a year. When we signed up with David Mackay to become the official Glenn Miller Orchestra, we stopped the Japanese tour in deference to Larry O'Brien's U.S. Glenn Miller Orchestra who had been serving that market. Glenn's music is powerful."

Ray McVay's musicians perform about 120 dates per year, about one every third day. "You know, Max, the cruise dates are nice as we remain in one place for six days and nights. No unpacking, a deserved rest for the band. At home, we perform at jazz festivals and castle concerts throughout Scotland and Ireland. We even go to Spain and South America."

Recruiting musicians is never a problem for Ray McVay. Most of the players have been with the band for years, so when one does leave, the spot is easily filled by another eager musician.

Becoming a "Glenn Miller Orchestra"

"When we play 'Moonlight Serenade' with five saxes, it sounds okay. You add the lead clarinet and it becomes magic. When we play this almost hymn-like song, we can see people becoming sentimental, even crying, because this song brings back memories. "When we did the tour with Willie, Jimmy and Zeke, shortly after we received a call from David Mackay's office to inquire if we would be interested in organizing an official Glenn Miller Orchestra outside of America. Of course, I would! This, after all, was what I always wanted. I flew to New York and spent three days there, and we agreed to work together. I inquired if I would have access to copies of Glenn's original music, and they said: 'No problem.'

Ray McVay: *"After the war, some kind people packed up all of Glenn's music, stored it in waterproof hampers, and shipped it back to the States. It is all there in a vault and accessible. It is nice, Max. If I need the music to a particular song, I call David Mackay's office and a week later I have it, complete with Glenn's pencil marks and scribbles. It's fascinating. It will say, 'cut from here to there-use this kind of mute here, another there.' All these markings which Glenn put onto the notes. You can't ask for anything more than that."*

Having moved from New York to Florida, Glenn Miller Productions is where Ray McVay joins with David Mackay from time to time for a game of golf and some shop talk. For Ray McVay the audiences seem to have a thirst for Glenn Miller's music more than ever before. It's not on the radio as much as it used to be, so people attend the concerts more often than before. According to Ray, the people come to hear what they have missed for a long time-good music. They are enjoying it. They love the big band music. When the band's Moonlight Serenaders sing "I've got a Gal in Kalamazoo," and "Chattanooga Choo Choo," it is heaven for them, and absolutely heaven for the singers and the musicians as well. These are the great Glenn Miller classics that will always be played. But it is "Moonlight Serenade" that still receives the strongest and longest applause. "It's Glenn's own composition. And, at the end of this song, at the end of the concert, when the audience stands up and applauds, I always say, 'I wish Glenn could still be around and see that people still enjoy his immortal 'Moonlight Serenade.'"

Enclosed in her 2003 Christmas card to Richard Grudens, among other things, Patty Andrews, the last remaining member of the Andrews Sisters, wrote:

> "I am so glad you are writing about the great Glenn Miller bands. We shared in many Glenn Miller festivals in the 90's, especially in England with Ray McVay. Ray's band is the best of all the Glenn Miller bands over there. He is a good friend and I enjoyed singing with his band backing me at all those concerts."

Max's Magnificent
PLAYER INTERVIEWS

Aside from the wonderful stories of Wil Salden, John Miller, and Ray McVay, the European and English counterparts to Larry O'Brien's own Glenn Miller Orchestra, there remains a number of popular musicians who have been influenced, or maybe just touched, by the magic of Glenn Miller's music at one time or another in their professional careers.

BRYAN PENDLETON

> *"For us, the music in the* Glenn Miller Story *film became the trademark music of our lives."*

In April of 2003, Max sat down with Bryan Pendleton, band leader, piano player, and arranger of big band music, at the Easter Weekend Big Band Bash at the Sand Bay Holiday Village, Weston-Super-Mare near Bristol, England.

Brian explains the loneliness of a long distance piano player. "In the old days, working piano bars and hotel lobby's you sit in a corner of the room playing your heart out and nobody is listening. But, it had its creative moments too."

After working big bands in the 1950s, it became obvious to Bryan that the big bands were folding and dance halls became discos. However, earlier, when he was a teenager, he had heard Glenn Miller's music on some 78's he owned. *The Glenn Miller Story* film became the landmark, as hearing that music, brought it to his attention, and punctuated the difference from the sound of all the other bands.

"We bought arrangements from music stores, but they were bland, written for simple, straight forward music making. With encouragement from the sounds of leaders like Ted Heath, I listened to everything they played and learned, but in my own arrangements I added some salt and pepper to it. Every band sounds different than others. Glenn Miller's music with four instead of five saxophones and the clarinet lead was completely different.

"Miller wanted it mellow and sweet, so he came to the logical conclusion, that if he substituted an instrument that is pitched in the same key as a lead trumpet, he might get it. It was pretty obvious that the clarinet could do it. And, history tells that it fit perfectly. I tend to believe that it is the real reason for the clarinet lead."

From 1967, Bryan played with the Syd Lawrence band, that featured much Miller music, playing piano and arranging, for many years. Today, he plays with the Andy Prior organization. When he writes charts for Prior, he will not be asked to put in some Miller trademarks. Andy likes the period of Billy May, Ray Anthony, and Basie, and also Nelson Riddle. May, for Bryan, is somewhere between Glenn Miller and the 40s period brought forward into the 60s. "When Syd was in the RAF, he was a Miller fan and transcribed a lot of his music for the RAF Dance Band. It was logical to pick up the same style again in his civilian band during the late 60s. Syd always said the Miller music was easy on the ear, good to play, was musically rewarding, and the fellows enjoyed playing it. The public loved it, as the Miller music gets the strongest applause. They go home whistling or humming the tunes. You could play 'Sunny Side of the Street' and 'String of Pearls', for example, and the applause would be drastically different in favor of 'String of Pearls.'

"Oski Brunnschwiler has me write for him for the Old Fashion Big Band of Zurich. He will call to say, write me a couple of titles and please put a little clarinet lead into it. He always loves the Glenn Miller sound, so I put a little Miller into it, and have for over ten years. His musicians and his audiences are happy with Glenn Miller's music."

HAZY OSTERWALD

"He was a phenomena, overshadowing everything we had heard by other American bands."

Max Wirz and Hazy Osterwald have become friends. At the Hotel Grand National in Lucerne, Switzerland, the two got together for Hazy's association with Glenn's music. Details of his career appear in *The Music Men* published in 1998.

"Years before Glenn Miller brought his orchestra to England, we were listening to his U.S. civilian orchestra. He was a phenomena, overshadowing everything we had heard by other American bands.

"In 1942, I was in boot camp in the Swiss Army, and on Sunday's I went to the Congress House in Zurich, where Teddy Stauffer and his Original Teddies performed. I remember very well how they did 'Chattanooga Choo Choo.'

"At that time, the whole world was influenced by Glenn Miller, way back over 60 years ago. After the war I had my own band, and Sunny Lang, a bass player and singer, collected Miller records. He always had the scoop on Glenn Miller and acquired new records by him. After we saw *Sun Valley Serenade*, the whole band went back to see it three or four times. We learned a lot from the way the band and soloists presented themselves.

"When we all gathered around to hear the Glenn Miller Christmas show from Paris, you can imagine how sad we were to learn that he had perished just a few days earlier."

For Hazy Osterwald, Glenn's music was easy to listen to, and after hearing a tune, you could sing or hum it for hours, as many people confirm. Hazy would adapt Glenn's music for his own orchestra.

"The dancers asked for 'In the Mood,' 'Tuxedo Junction,' and 'Moonlight Serenade,' and would not let us go unless we also played 'Adios.' It was not easy to adapt the arrangements that were written for a seventeen piece band to even our sextet or slightly larger group. But, we did it, and the people loved us for it."

For Hazy Osterwald, Europe's great musical icon, who is now eighty-two years old and still working, Glenn's music was a true phenomenon, a one in a million success that has lasted. Whenever he is a guest with a big band, there are Glenn Miller melodies included in his repertoire.

"I am sure there will be more of the same in 2004, Glenn's centenary. When we do these songs with small bands, however, it is difficult to sound Miller-like, but I am sure I will perform some songs on vibes, with the sextet, and as a guest with the full size Dani Felber Big Band.

DANI FELBER

"I am happy to say, I have come a long way, thanks to Glenn Miller."

Talking with Dani Felber was a repeat for Max Wirz. Max had encountered Dani when he was a teenager, playing cornet at a birthday party. This young man at the age of 32 has since then toured Europe with his own combo Jazz Dependents, playing more than 200 concerts, then graduating to his own big band in 2000, despite friendly advice not to do it. The band is composed of professional musicians mostly fresh from known jazz schools and directed by Dani, an extraordinary and dedicated leader at the dawn of a long and rewarding career.

"I was about nine when my mother gave me a tape of Glenn Miller playing all the famous charts like, 'Chattanooga Choo Choo,' and 'In the Mood,' all those beautiful masterpieces. I became a fan right away and listened to the tape over and over. The I saw *The Glenn Miller Story* and set a goal for myself to copy this man and to some day stand

Dani Felber

on stage in front of my own band. Today, years later, I have my own Big Band, work with musicians on and with my own arrangements, looking, not unlike Glenn, for my own sound. I am happy to say, I have come a long way, thanks to Glenn Miller.

Dani had received music lessons in local brass societies, playing marches and orchestral arrangements, having no idea of jazz or big band music until he received that tape cassette. Listening to those tapes compelled Dani to try his luck with a band, like Glenn did at first. "Glenn Miller had his clarinet led saxophone section and his trombone section. Then there were composers and arrangers, men like Miller who had conceptions on how their music had to sound. Unfortunately, this is almost impossible today. Although having my own band, I am fortunate in that I can write and arrange special pieces for my musicians, like Glenn Miller once did."

Dani's band plays mixed material, but also performs specials. During the forthcoming Fall Fair [October 03] they intend to present two Glenn Miller Nights exclusively with the Miller sound. Dani reassures Max that on October 18, 2003, the Dani Felber Big Band will celebrate the Swiss German Dixie Corporation's 25th Year Jubilee with Max as MC, where they will play a few Miller tunes. New, young bands in Europe, like Dani Felber's Big Band, help carry the torch for Glenn's revered music, insuring its continuity throughout this century.

HUGO STRASSER

"Glenn Miller is a man who gave us such wonderful, everlasting music."

Hugo Strasser, clarinet player and orchestra leader, grew up and studied music in Munich, Germany, when World

War II broke out. Like Paul Kuhn, Bert Kaempfert, and Max Greger, were leaders of dance bands, which in the '50s, '60s, and '70s appeared regularly on German radio and television stations, and toured throughout the country performing concerts and dances.

"In 1944 in Munich, I was 22 years old. Jazz and American music was forbidden in Germany. But, we secretly listened to this new music over 'sender' from France and England. Around that time I heard recordings of Glenn Miller and his civilian orchestra as well as his Army band and it fascinated me."

Hugo Strasser

Then, in 1944, Hugo Strasser had no idea that in less than two years he would actually be playing that music. When the war was over he got the chance to become acquainted with American soldiers and was soon performing in their service clubs. He remembered how perplexed the GIs were that they knew their music and were able to play it.

"The Glenn Miller sound was foremost, the saxophone section and how he put the clarinet in the lead. And then those trombones with their doo-wha, doo-wha. For us this was fascinating and we played with indescribable enthusiasm. Imagine, Max, we had survived a terrible war, and then suddenly we were allowed to play music, which was previously forbidden. It was like swinging on a cloud. It was the beginning of music as a profession for many of us." Of course, Hugo Strasser played the music of many other big bands that were popular at the time, but Glenn Miller's music was the most influential. Hugo's piano players played like Duke Ellington, and their trumpet player emulated Harry James, and so forth. They could not reach their perfection, but they sure tried. Because Hugo played the clarinet, the GIs called him Benny, after Benny Goodman. But, it was the Miller music that showed them a definitive direction.

"We graduated from there, and in 1948, we were hired by hotels and night clubs, a mixed audience of GIs and local citizens. Radio discovered us and so did television. We moved along step by step and adapted and perfected our music style. Over the years, many of those great American musicians came over to Europe and we had the chance to meet them, even jam with them in our clubs. You cannot imagine what these meetings meant to us."

Another thrill was felt by Hugo Strasser who, with Ray Anthony, wrote a composition, "Lonely Trumpet" later played by Ray Anthony. Although he received no money for it, he didn't mind. It was important to Hugo that an American star was playing his composition.

"During 2004, we will continue doing concerts in large and small cities of Germany. In each we have a Miller section with 'In the Mood', 'American Patrol,' and 'Moonlight Serenade.' We have to play these, no matter how often we have played them before. The highlight of each concert is the playing of 'In the Mood,' a song that will remain popular through this century, I am fully convinced. You cannot replace the Glenn Miller music with any other music. Glenn Miller is a man who gave us such wonderful, everlasting music.

PEPE LIENHARD

"To play Glenn Miller so that it really sounds like Miller, requires a whole lot of skill and discipline."

Pepe Lienhard has been a musician and band leader since his teens. His fourteen piece show and pop orchestra and his seventeen piece swing band are known all over Europe. Along with vocalist Udo Jurgens, who has sold 70 million albums worldwide, Pepe Lienhard's band will perform with Udo in dozens of concert halls all over Europe during 2004.

"The Glenn Miller Orchestra was the first big band which I recognized as such. 'Moonlight Serenade,' heard on Swiss

---

Radio, was my first experience with that sound. That was the mid fifties, when I was about ten."

When Pepe heard the Miller tunes "Tuxedo Junction," and "In the Mood," he was electrified, especially after being exposed to rock and roll for a while. He was fascinated with the clarinet lead as many other musicians before him. When he viewed *Sun Valley Serenade* and *Orchestra Wives*, he noticed the superb stage presence, and swung right along with the music. "It was great entertainment, too. These frolicking, swinging tunes made the kids kick up their heels and those soft ballads were balm for the lonely and homesick. It has not been easy to motivate young musicians to play Miller songs. Their enthusiasm grew only as we got down to the details and fine tuning. Musicians tend to underestimate the Miller music, because it sounds so simple and seems easy to play. Anyone can play Miller pieces, but to play things like 'Moonlight Serenade' so that it really sounds like an original Miller, requires a whole lot of skill and discipline.

Pepe Lienhard

"But, Glenn Miller played hundreds of other numbers not in the special Miller sound, but still arranged and played to perfection. Such achievements are possible only with the best arrangers and best musicians."

Pepe Lienhard wasn't over-influenced by Glenn's music, but, he knew, that as a bandleader you could not ignore Glenn Miller's charts. However, when the Swiss Army Band, under his direction, plays Miller tunes, and with Sammi Zund and his fellow singers of the Swing-4-U go into their Modernaires routine, they always receive the strongest and longest applause, everywhere for every audience.

"For 2004 we have two projects planned which will feature Glenn Miller music, each involving concert tours through Switzerland and Germany. The seventeen piece Pepe Leinhard Orchestra will perform a special Glenn Miller Gala Show."

PAUL KUHN

"The very first recording I ever heard was by the Glenn Miller Orchestra."

Paul Kuhn

Germany's seventy-five year old Paul Kuhn, profiled in the book *Jukebox Saturday Night* is a much revered bandleader and entertainer. Still active throughout Germany, his musical ensemble will have played over one hundred concerts in 2003-4. He feels he owes a lot to Glenn Miller.

"The very first recording I heard was by the Glenn Miller Orchestra. It was a kind of music that was totally unfamiliar to me, but it made a very big impression. So, I became a big band fan—and still am today.

"The Miller Army Air Corps band came to England during the war. I had heard a previous recording of 'Anvil Chorus', not recorded in the typical Miller sound, but I had a hankering for operatic melodies and thought it was special and different, although it was 'jazzed up' and in the opinion of the time, played in an unworthy way. We would listen to those BBC broadcasts with the American Band of the Expeditionery Force with Glenn Miller and Ilse Weinberger. We also heard Artie Malvin and the Crew Chiefs, Bing Crosby, Johnny Desmond, Dinah Shore, Ray McKinley, and Irene Manning. Officials were directing their programs at the youth of Germany. The singers sang German texts phonetically-Diese Musik hat mich einfach umgehauen! The

---

music knocked me over." Paul knew that if someday he ever was allowed to play this kind of music, he would become a jazz musician, thanks to Glenn Miller. His colleagues Hugo Strasser, Max Greger, and Hazy Osterwald had similar feelings when they first heard Glenn. Paul fully appreciates the sound created by Glenn, and considers it a fabulous invention on the basis of his success.

At the beginning of 2004, Paul Kuhn and his group will perform enriched Glenn Miller programs, which are already sold out in palaces like the Friedrichstadt in Berlin with 2,300 seats. Recently the performances there were sold out five consecutive evenings.

"In the 50s, 60s, and 70s, when we did our TV shows, or when we played at dances with the Paul Kuhn Orchestra and the Ute Mann Singers, we played so much Miller, that all of us had more than enough of it. Each of us must have played 'In the Mood' two thousand times in our careers. But the audience never tires of it and promoters and record companies insisted on the Glenn Miller Sound."

For Paul Kuhn, with Glenn Miller musical material implanted in his brain for so long, he feels he can not help it when Glenn Miller material absorbs into new things and new arrangements.

BILLY GORLT

"It was a sound we had not heard up until that time, the way it was put together, the special blend, it was amazing to us."

At Billy and Irene Gorlt's home, after a perfect dinner, Max Wirz and Billy Gorlt exchange Glenn Miller conversations.

"After obtaining my wings in glider school, I was transferred to a heavy mortar unit North of Frankfurt. Then, on my 18th birthday, I was taken prisoner by advancing American units, and wound up in a camp in France a few days later. I was on detail to help transport wounded American soldiers and one of them had a Hohner accordion tied to his stretcher.

Max and Billy

I played it and learned American songs, becoming pretty popular. "Billy received lessons from a fellow POW, who was a musician before the war. He played in the POW band that performed at the officers Club. He got interested in the clarinet and saxophone. Still a POW in 1947, Billy played in a big band managed by a U.S. Sergeant, but staffed by POWs. By this time he became a good sight reader on clarinet and saxophone.

"We played printed arrangements of popular U.S. swing music charts received through Special Services. Oh, Max, those beautiful songs: 'In the Mood,' 'Moonlight Serenade,' and all the Dorsey and Harry James, Count Basie, and more charts...all the great music of the Swing Era. My self taught skills became a great advantage and earned me a spot in a club that was crowed seven nights a week."

When freed, Billy joined a circus band for a while and eventually secured a job and continued to play for American military right up to 1967, from 1960 under his own name with his own quartet. Looking back, Billy remembered hearing the strains of "Moonlight Serenade" and "In the Mood."

"It was a smooth and beautiful melody. It was a big band with that wonderful sound everyone talked about. We were all surprised at the simplicity of the melodies and beat. It was overwhelming, simply overwhelming. I thought, if they have such good music, they must be good people."

When Billy got to listen to Glenn's music, he noticed how carefully Glenn Miller had selected the music, melodies and rhythms. He would go from one different song to another, different in tempo, different in instrumentation and in sound.

"For me, Glenn was a good organizer of his material, and he knew what people wanted to hear and he gave it to them. His perfection in music is what impressed me so. The arrangers wrote catchy introductions for each song. He was a stickler, a perfectionist, but he was successful. When we play Glenn Miller, *we play Glenn Miller."*

Viewing the *Glenn Miller Story* film gave Billy Gorlt the idea to wear U.S. uniforms on stage. The audience went wild when they played "Tuxedo Junction" at the Prinzregenten Theater in Munich, Germany. It was like scenes from the movie, when Glenn played in hangars to GI audiences back in England in 1944.

"In 2004, in memory of Glenn Miller, we will do a special program in the Stadthalle of Germering next Spring. There will be five tunes for a vocal group. They sing like the Modernaires. We will be sold out. And, we are recording the entire program on a CD which will be called 'Billy Gorlt and the Airforce Band, Volume 2.'"

OSKAR "OSKI" BRUNNSCHWILER

"It's the quality of the Glenn Miller arrangements and soloists and singers who made a deep impression on me."

A thirty-seven year veteran of Zurich's police force, Oskar Brunnschwiler began his musical career in the Knabenmusik Zurich, the Boys Brass Band Corps of Zurich, playing tenor horn, and now plays clarinet and saxophone, as well as Hammond Organ, performing up to seventy concerts a year in many private events.

"Oski," as he is known, and three fellow musicians, founded the Old Fashion Big Band of Zurich, and, now associated with Bryan Pendleton of England, who arranges his music with Miller sounds, the band regularly plays those Miller standards.

Born in 1937, Oski listened to Swiss National Radio where he heard Glenn Miller's music. He would save his money to go downtown in Zurich to buy an occasional record or two. He played a second hand saxophone, and later a clarinet, earned by working at odd jobs after school. At twenty-five, he became a Hammond Organ fan and learned to play it quite well.

"Music is important to my life. Glenn Miller's straight forward melodies, played with gusto and precision, made a deep impression on me. I also admired the big bands of Fred Boehler and Hazy Osterwald in Switzerland."

Oski enjoys the soft sounds of Glenn Miller and the sax section with the clarinet lead that is so famous. Bryan Pendleton told Max Wirz that when Oski asks for an arrangement, he always requests "a little Miller" in it. Max always describes it on his Radio Eviva show as "dancing as in Glenn Miller's times."

"For 2004, we will follow our regular formula of playing a lot of Glenn Miller songs, and will continue to perform that beautiful big band sound, as Max suggests on Radio Eviva broadcasts, for dancing as in Glenn Miller's time."

ANDY PRIOR

"Whenever we strike up a Miller song, the audience peps up."

Andy Prior

Andy Prior's first connection to Glenn Miller was listening to Glenn's trombone section's boo-ba, boo-ba, boo-ba, and for him, that was enough influence. Andy was but six years old.

"I also remember the album cover sleeve with Glenn and his rimless glasses, because my dad wore them too."

The effect was that Andy wanted to be a leader like Glenn, and he wanted to sing like Frank Sinatra or Mel Tormé. For him, the Glenn Miller band was the one name in music that has created more employment for musicians than any other big band.

"Yet it's not the easiest of music to play correctly, but whenever we strike up a Miller song, the audience peps up. I think Syd Lawrence orchestrated new material in the Miller way, coming close to the original sound. Today, Chris Dean is using some of the AEF material as he fronts Syd's orchestra. But, it's 'In the Mood,' 'Tuxedo Junction,' and 'Moonlight Serenade' that the people want to hear, always." Andy Prior has toured with The Magic of Sinatra tour throughout England with his own band, went to America in 2002 to front the Billy May Orchestra ghost band at the Stardust Hotel in Las Vegas, playing Billy's charts, and went back to Las Vegas and performed with Ray Anthony's band. "While I was there, we had a reunion with Ray, Johnny Best, Paul Tanner, and Billy May. It was a great experience."

FREDDY STAFF

"The eternal success of 'Moonlight Serenade' proves Glenn's music will always be played somewhere forever."

Freddy Staff, trumpet player and leader of his own orchestra and the Manhattan Swing Orchestra as well, in England, encountered Glenn Miller music for the first time during World War II.

"I was about 13 years old. The Glenn Miller band was here and we heard it over the AFN radio broadcasts. After the war I got a Miller record, 'Moonlight Serenade. I was playing the bugle in the Boy Scouts." At fifteen, Freddy entered a Harry James contest and won first prize, ten Shillings.

Freddy Staff
(Max Wirz collection)

As a teenager he played in a local band, then in 1946 he played with the Royal Air Force band, until 1949. Upon his discharge, he attended the College of Music to receive teacher's qualification. Freddy played in the orchestra on the cruise ship, Queen Mary, making 12 trips to New York. When in New York, he took twelve trumpet lessons from noted instructor Benny Baker.

"I try to play like Harry James. I was initially impressed with Harry when he played in the film *Two Girls and a Sailor.* Boy, that was trumpet playing. I was dumb struck. I was playing trombone, so I switched back to trumpet. I began to emulate Harry's style. He was a 'pop' star. I would look in the mirror and imitate the way he blew. He did not puff his cheeks out and he kept his lips close together. But, that was in films. In reality, he puffed his cheeks out, too.'

Getting back to Glenn's music, Max, searched Freddy's memory:

"I think it was the sound, that saxophone sound with the clarinet lead, not the brass. It was so simple to score, it's close harmony, you've got the clarinet on top. It's so effective, and a marvelous trade mark for Miller fans. The success of 'Moonlight Serenade' proves it. The public wants a dance, so Miller is essential. Lately, I have started to do a Miller Medley, a few titles strung together. Our version of 'American Patrol' is with a little bit of the famous Marine Hymn added. I like doing Glenn Miller, but people know me and we do a bit of our own material, and they accept it."

WIEBE SCHUURMANS

> *"I think it is fantastic that Glenn Miller's music continues to succeed."*

Wiebe Schuurmans is seventy-four and plays clarinet and saxophone in the Glenn Miller Orchestra directed by Wil Salden, and sings as a member of the Moonlight Serenaders, the modern Modernaires, and has been with Wil's band since 1991.

At sixteen, after the war in Holland, while Wiebe's father worked in a dairy, he played soprano saxophone. When he was at work, Wiebe secretly learned to play that instrument.

"After the war, I joined an orchestra that had three accordions, one alto sax, and drums. My father did not like that. He wanted me to fulfill myself in a proper occupation. But later, when he saw and heard me play in the Radio Orchestra, he became very proud and happy." "The musicians in the Radio Orchestra played swing music. During the war we heard American swing music over the BBC, but, listening to such music was 'verboten' (forbidden). Then, in 1945, during victory parties, we had dancers hopping with 'In the Mood,' 'My Guys Come Back,' and the difficult for us to do, 'Moonlight Serenade.'"

For Wiebe, the influential music of Glenn Miller was mixed with the music of many American bands. From his early days, Wiebe Schuurmans played in many bands throughout Holland and Europe. He played clarinet in the Miller Sextet, and the Flamingo Quintet (a kind of Shearing band where the guitar is substituted with the clarinet).

Wiebe was offered a job with the Dutch Metropole Radio Orchestra and grabbed it, and started playing baritone saxophone remaining with it until 1991. While with the sixty piece symphonic orchestra, that included a big band, he also helped out Wil Salden a few times. When he retired from the Radio Orchestra, he joined his now good friend, Wil Salden for keeps. At seventy four, Wiebe manages to play over 200 one nighter's each year.

"I love it. The Glenn Miller Orchestra is well known throughout Europe, playing the music people want to hear. The band is well managed and we travel in a comfortable bus and stay at good hotels. We all love it. The concerts are two hours and sometimes even longer. Sometimes it gets tiring, but, all in all, it's wonderful." Max wondered if Wiebe ever gets bored being on stage evening after evening, opening with "Moonlight Serenade," and closing with "Adios," and "In the Mood" for the encore?

Wiebe: "Every concert is a new concert. Sometimes the folks are cool and hard to warm up. It's a challenge. Together with Wil, the girl singer and two other musicians, I am a member of the Moonlight Serenaders, doing the Miller songs. I get a chance, to play solos and while on center stage, I seek eye to eye contact with someone in the audience and clown around a little.

"I think it is fantastic how Glenn's music continues to succeed. It is astounding how many people come to our concerts, year after year, and, as they grow older they bring their children and grandchildren to hear our Glenn Miller music."

STEVE KING

"When they ask for Miller tunes, we do them and they love us for it."

Steve King, trumpet player with his own big band, met Max at Sand Bay Holiday Village near Bristol, England, on April 20, 2003.

"We mostly play contemporary music at our concerts, like the music of Bob Florence and Tom Cubis, but when we are at dance dates we play Glenn Miller music. The dancers will sometimes sit out a dance or two, and, when they ask for Miller tunes, naturally 'In the Mood,' 'Moonlight Serenade,' 'American Patrol', 'Serenade in Blue,' and 'Adios'—we do them and they love us for it."

Steve King plays swing music with his big band at Pontin's Pakefield and Potter's in Hopton on Sea, on the East Coast of England. He recalls the influence Glenn's music had on his later work. Now in his 33rd year and with his own band, Steve explains his early encounter with Glenn's music:

"It was in the mid-seventies when I got into playing trumpet and wanted to play in a big band. Everyone related to the Glenn Miller sound, and we trumpet players, were especially intrigued by the trumpet solos. I listened to records of the original Miller band and, encouraged by this great music, went to listen to English big bands, like the Syd Lawrence Orchestra. I learned a lot from listening to these two great orchestras."

THILO WOLF

"I would never dream to rearrange 'Moonlight Serenade.' That piece is perfect."

Thilo Wolf, pianist, drummer, composer, arranger, big band leader, was born in 1967. When he was but twelve, his father was a friend of Klaus Wunderlich, the famous organist who played the Hammond, and would bring over American recordings of Glenn Miller and other artists when he would visit him.

Thilo Wolf

"As I recall very clearly, I thought 'Don't Sit Under the Apple Tree' was a real swinging number. Those records and the records of Max Greger and his Orchestra, was my first contact with the big bands.

"I played some of those themes on the piano and learned them by heart. Then I saw *The Glenn Miller Story* on TV and liked it very much. But, what impressed more was the dance scenes in the first Miller film, *Sun Valley Serenade*. That's when the Miller virus got me."

To Thilo Wolf, Glenn Miller's orchestra was the most popular band of his era, too, because he felt the simple melodies Glenn featured were ones you could whistle after hearing them just once.

"And the Miller sax section with clarinet brought an unmistakable element. The fantastic arrangements, created by a number of innovative arrangers, were unique. Take 'Little Brown Jug.' Such a simple melody and wonderful arrangement. The secret probably does not lie in any one of those details but rather in the combination of them all."

Thilo plays Glenn Miller from available standard arrangements. He will take Glenn Miller material, but interpret it in his own way.

Thilo and his band.
(courtesy Thilo Wolf)

"Jazz is melody, harmony and rhythm. You can vary the melody only a little, but you can use various rhythms to obtain variety. However, I would never dream of rewriting 'Moonlight Serenade,' a piece that is perfect. Miller melodies put every crowd 'In the Mood.' When I was sixteen, we played Basie and Neil Hefti. We discussed whether Miller should be played at all. It was our youthful inexperience to almost taboo Miller, not wanting to play the old stuff which had been played a hundred, thousand times. We did not want to play easy tunes. But, today I know that it is very difficult to play these easy Miller songs so that they sound like Miller. And we have learned to respect that there were, and have been, millions of listeners who simply adored and still adore this music."

Thilo Wolf is considering the use of Glenn Miller and his music to be part of Swing 2004.

"Let us surprise you next March." He said in parting.

FRANK TOUHEY

> *"They have to play Miller music,*
> *because the people ask for it."*

Frank Touhey, who founded Montpellier Records, is an expert on the big bands of both England and America. His company is a most valid base of operations for the distribution of big band music in England. The company is now managed by his son, Kevin. Sales of recordings by Ray Anthony, who has a good feeling for what the public wants, records much of his music based on the Glenn Miller sound, especially in the Dream Dancing Series that features the sound of the Glenn Miller saxophone section. His records sell well year after year. Anthony maintains his own record distribution business in California.

> *Frank Touhey: "We first received Miller scores when I was playing clarinet and saxophone in a dance band back in 1942. We had heard his music on the radio, then we saw Sun Valley Serenade and Orchestra Wives where the band was featured. I think viewing those films got the whole thing rolling in the UK."*

Frank Touhey and Bryan Pendleton with Max Wirz

In April, 1944, the AEF band arrived in England and began broadcasting on the BBC. Because of the many numbers of broadcasts, it almost became a British Orchestra. Everyone in England was listening to the Glenn Miller Orchestra.

"In 1944 the Miller band was actually stationed in Bedford, about 12 miles from my home. I was sixteen and took a bus to Bedford and tried to get in during a rehearsal, but they wouldn't let me in. Then an American Top Sergeant came to the door and invited me in. That Sergeant was Ray McKinley. Forty years later on a Big Band Jump cruise I shook hands with Ray and told him that story. He said, 'Wow, I never knew I was such a nice guy.'

"For Frank Touhey, the whaa whaa of the trombones and the smooth mix of saxophone and clarinet lead was suitable for war time listening conditions. It had people thinking about loved ones who were away from home. Now, sixty years later, the music remains popular in England and America.

"In all my years in the music business, the conversation always turned to Glenn Miller and his fabulous sound. To many, the sound of Miller at dances is the sound of big band and dance music. Others have tried with mixed success. The saxophone lead with the muted trumpets identify the great Miller charts, and we featured this music when I was playing with the RAF band."

A Glenn Miller Society was formed in England with members all over the country. They had four meetings a year in London, and members would give recitals, spin records, and tell stories about Miller and associated musicians. The Society remains active today. Steven Miller is the president and Richard March is secretary. Telephone is Verwood (01202) 825692 and located at 3 Pine View Close, Dorset, England.

"People do associate happenings in their lives with Miller music, either consciously or not. They talk about how they met their wives at a Miller dance. This holds true to the actual Glenn Miller era, but also to the later years, during which the great English Big Bands were, and are still, touring the country.

COLIN GOODALL

"His songs made us walk away whistling, which you cannot do with today's music."

Colin Goodall, an amateur drummer, sometime CD engineer for Montpellier Records, operates with a computer and modern software to take old recordings and clean them up for mastering and eventual production, loves the big bands.

Max spoke to him in England during the Easter Weekend Big Band Bash of April, 2003.

"In the '50s The Glenn Miller Story hit England. I remember one afternoon I went to the cinema and stayed for six performances, all the way through, again and again. Not enough, the following week I went two more times. It was wonderful and great music. Henry Mancini arranged the music in the film, but it was Glenn's sound that gave so much splendid music to the world: melody, rhythm, and songs that made us walk away whistling, which we are unable to do with today's music. That was the music I was raised on, the Glenn Miller Orchestra."

PART SIX

THE GLENN MILLER
ORCHESTRA OF TODAY

Westhampton Beach, NY - July 2003

Today's Glenn Miller Orchestra

On July 27, 2003, along with colleague, photographer, and wife, Madeline, I got together with Larry O'Brien once again for an all day and evening interview and overview of the Glenn Miller Orchestra at the freshly restored Westhampton Beach Performing Arts Center in New York, before a scheduled concert. In Larry's dressing room, after exchanging greetings and inquiries about past friends

(Madeline Grudens photo)

whereabouts and adventures, he conversed readily about his current batch of nineteen stellar musicians and the state of today's Glenn Miller Orchestra.

"Some of the more modern parts of our repertoire we play in the big band style. Some we don't. What we're trying to do is run this band the way we feel Glenn would have if he were still here. You know, music is sometimes deceiving.

"It may be simple in that the notes aren't that hard or that high or that fast, but I've always been of the opinion that simple music is the hardest to play. It's easy to put up a smoke screen with flashy music, but to play something really simple—together, everybody in tune, blending—is quite hard.

"A lot of kids have become enthralled by what they hear. We've got some hot players on the stand who can really perform. I think our appeal will keep growing—especially with the kids who love our kind of music."

Aside from his skill as a leader who drives this young, sparkling band, Larry is a brilliant trombonist. His solo version of "Danny Boy" that I witnessed him playing during our visit, regularly captivates the crowd. His Dorsey breath-control style playing is dominated by those long legato phrases, so smooth, clean and perfect. His own musicians admire him greatly, which helps produce a unified group, much like Glenn managed to provide so successfully back in the early forties.

The consensus that Glenn Miller's music legacy will continue into the 21st century, prompted Larry O'Brien to state:

> *"It seems that good things just don't ever die. Rather, they age gracefully with the years. If anything, Richard, I honestly think the authentic Glenn Miller music is more popular today with more people than ever before. Just look out at that full house tonight. The Glenn Miller legacy remains with us."*

And, it's interesting to note, that on August 16, 2003, some 60 years later, like a happy ghost, the Glenn Miller Orchestra returned to one of their very early venues, a place where the band first earned its wings on the road to their mercurial success, The legendary Meadowbrook Ballroom in Cedar Grove, on New Jersey's Pompton Turnpike.

The Meadowbrook was one of the prestigious ballrooms where the cream of the big bands were featured, and from where they would broadcast those live performances, earning them all eternal fame. During the Westhampton Beach concert, a full standing ovation greeted the orchestra by both young and older fans after performing the opening and closing haunting strains of Glenn's legendary musical gem, "Moonlight Serenade." There were a lot of weepy eyes out there, too, including mine, as I sat among the faithful.

Today's Glenn Miller Orchestra, under the baton of its dedicated director, Larry O'Brien, travels worldwide to dispense its great musical charts, which now number over 1600, to more than a half-million enthusiastic fans annually, fulfilling the band's contracted itinerary that stretches across the oceans of the continents West to Japan and East, across the Atlantic, to Europe and beyond.

Stateside, the orchestra travels thousands of miles each month to fulfill their concert obligations, winding their way

Glenn Miller Director
Larry Obrien

(Madeline Grudens photo)

by bus throughout our land, crisscrossing every state in the forty-eight.

Today's band consists of Four trumpets, Five Trombones, Five Saxes (doubles on clarinet, flute), Piano, Bass, Drums, and two vocalists.

The musicians, much like in the early days, are mostly young and unattached and like to travel and perform one-night stands. Today, the buses contain massive improvements over the past. There is air-conditioning and television. Members of the orchestra originate from many different places:

Kevin Sheehan—Alto Clarinet, comes from Chicago. Matt Johns—plays alto sax and hails from Florida. Serafin Sanchez—is tenor One from Colorado. Philip Whack—is tenor saxist from South Carolina. Chad Gridley—plays baritone sax and comes from Ohio.

On trumpets are Ashley Hall—lead—from Florida, Mike Harrison—split lead—from Arizona, Alcedrick Todd plays third—jazz trumpet from Lousiana, and Jeff Smith is from Pennsylvania.

The trombone players, besides **Larry O'Brien**, who hails from Long Island, are **George Reinert III** from Alaska, **Doug Kost** from Pennslyvania, **Josh Favors** from Michigan and **Jimmy Borowski** from Pennsylvania. Pianist **Andy Nevala**, today's Chummy MacGreger, is from Indiana. The drums are hammered on by **Greg Parnell**. Don't forget **Shawn Marko**, the bass player from Ohio. Great musicians all, regardless of age. Larry O'Brien showcases one and all, singularly and doubly, over and over throughout each performance.

We interviewed some of his young musicians, including a revealing conversation with Illionois bred Kevin Sheehan, lead alto and singing member of the Moonlight Serenaders, the current name of the four man and one girl singing group, reminiscent of the Modernaires. Kevin's goal, to someday become a band leader, punctuated the dedication among all the players. Kevin recently celebrated six years with the band.

Simply, Larry O'Brien, a very dedicated musician, requires of his players what his predecessor, Glenn Miller, once did: Excellent musicianship, dedication to the band in performance, dress code, and showing up on time.

Good life, great music.

Kevin Sheehan, Lynn LaVigna, Nick Hilscher, Matt Johns and James Borowski
(Madeline Grudens photo)

Nick Hilscher - Vocalist
Today's Glenn Miller Orchestra

What a talented vocalist is Nick Hilscher. Nick, an amiable and personable young man of twenty-six with a solid presence, good looks, wise and responsible beyond his years with a perfect attitude, is headed for an even more solid future.

"I'm lucky. What an honor to work with this great band, what is now six years and counting. It's a joy to sing the music I learned to love, and Larry allows me a little space to do some of the vocals my own way. Larry's trombone playing totally inspires me, so all of this has been a great experience. Have you heard his trombone on 'Mamselle,' featured on my new CD, or 'Danny Boy,' that he does at our concerts."

Larry is thoroughly satisfied with Nick as the band's boy singer, as Glenn was happy with Ray Eberle. Watching Nick, who sings and phrases much like Ray, but sounds more like the richer baritone of Dick Haymes, particularly on his recordings of "Shine On Harvest Moon," and "How Deep is the Ocean," and whose presence on stage emulates the budding Sinatra, indeed, a throwback to the forties when male vocalists were an integral part of most big bands; Bing Crosby with Paul Whiteman, Sinatra and Dick Haymes with Tommy Dorsey, Joe Williams with Count Basie, Bob Eberly with Jimmy Dorsey, and Ray Eberle with Glenn.

When Nick viewed the film *The Glenn Miller Story* in 1989, he was but twelve. He had discovered Glenn's music and thereby a hopeful future for himself as a singer with a band, never thinking he would actually sing with the Glenn Miller Orchestra. Nick began by emulating the singing style and stage presence of Frank Sinatra, just as Sinatra once did with Bing Crosby, the father, he said, of his career.

A piano playing performance major in college, Nick sent a demo tape of his singing voice to Larry O'Brien. Nick was accepted at once when Larry and band vocalist Julia Rich heard his voice. He instantly became the Glenn Miller Orchestra boy singer in 1998. Nick returned to college the following year to complete his degree. After graduating, he returned to the singing chores of the orchestra, his great dream.

> *"We work 48 weeks a year, including over one month in Japan, touring to the delight of so many Glenn Miller fans. And, I love the responses we receive at home, particularly from the older fans who have enjoyed Glenn's recordings for so many years. Performing for them is an honor."*

When I caught up with Nick and the band in late July of 2003, I was able to personally witness the joy transcended to the listener when Nick performed "At Last" and "A Nightingale Sang in Berkeley Square," while rehearsing, and at the performance before a full theater. Nick doubles as band sound man, working closely with Larry O'Brien to establish sound checks in a given theater or venue before each show.

Nick has produced his own CD, "Nick Hilscher, with The Glenn Miller Orchestra," with Larry O'Brien's blessings and personal direction, and starring today's entire Glenn Miller Orchestra. Nick's enthusiastic dad, Bill Hilscher, directs Nick's career from their home in Marietta, Georgia, making certain disc jockey's and other interested people recieve CDs or related promotional material that will further the career of his talented son.

Dr. Paul Tanner, of Glenn Miller Orchestra fame, hailed Nick's CD, saying,"It is rare today to find a young man who sounds so great and looks great. Nick Hilscher keeps the wonderful Glenn Miller sounds alive and well."

JULIA RICH - Vocalist

Julia Rich's first performance with the Glenn Miller Orchestra was in 1985, at the Opryland Hotel in Nashville, Tennessee. Julia, a preacher's daughter from Nashville, has since become the featured female vocalist for the orchestra. Over the last almost 20 years, she has been touring through every state in the union, the Canadian Provinces, Spain, South America and even Japan. As an aspiring singer, Julia was much encouraged by her mother and father, Reverend Fred, and June Blankenship. She literally grew up singing in church choirs and at revivals conducted by her dad. With a Bachelor of Music degree, she picked up harmony singing from the Methodist hymnal and a fondness for the voice of Judy Garland. For her, voice lessons were helpful, and with a feeling for jazz, she turned to the sounds of the great Sarah Vaughan and legendary Billie Holiday, but the best instructions received turned out to be listening to premier vocalist Ella Fitzgerald on a pair of headphones. The direct, intense concentration directed Ella's spirited voice permanently into Julia's psyche. Feeling a divine spark, Julia became uplifted by Ella's phrasing principles.

Today, Julia Rich enjoys performing in the many beautiful, old theaters, opera houses, and high School auditoriums throughout the country, full of friendly people who enjoy good music. It constantly encourages and inspires her. Watching couples that have danced together for 50 years and listening to them muse about what the music meant to them early in their lives together enriches her feelings for the great music the Glenn Miller Orchestra perpetuates. While singing with the orchestra, Julia has been fortunate to have performed with The Mills Brothers, Rosemary Clooney, Jerry Vale, Connie Haines, and other great voices that preceded her own career. Julia has received invaluable inspiration and encouragement from Dr. Paul Tanner, of the original civilian Glenn Miller Orchestra, and Irene Wolf, Glenn's sister, who was a cherished friend.

From time to time, Julia sings with a small group and sometimes just a piano or guitar, making music with many worthy musicians over the years. Larry O'Brien considers Julia Rich to be one of the best Glenn Miller Orchestra vocalists ever. Along the way, Julia Rich has recorded two albums for Cardinal Records: "I'll Take Romance," and "The Way You Make Me Feel."

A worthy voice for the great Glenn Miller book of songs.

The Glenn Miller Birthplace Society

The Glenn Miller Birthplace Society was organized in 1976 and currently lists over 1700 members in 47 States and twenty-four foreign countries, with a branch formed in Tokyo, Japan in 1993.

Glenn's daughter, Jonnie Miller, purchased her dad's 1904 Clarinda, Iowa birthplace home in 1989. A major restoration of the homesite was undertaken in 1991. A 1912 addition was removed and the original roof line restored, among other detailed changes, carefully restoring it to the original design. Luckily, a fellow named Bob Watson proved to be helpful in the restoration process, as his parents had purchased the home from Glenn's parents in 1907. His memory and the photos he provided kept the process more authentic.

The stated goal of the Glenn Miller Foundation is to improve and maintain the home so that it may be enjoyed by its countless visitors the world over. They invite everyone to donate funds to this noble effort in preserving the vintage home. The non-profit foundation is located at 122 West Garfield, Clarinda, Iowa 51632.

Membership in the Glenn Miller Birthplace Society is twenty-five dollars with various options. They produce a quarterly newsletter that provides information about society activities that include the annual June festival held in Clarinda. In 2004, the event will be held on June 12 through the 15th and will feature Larry O'Brien and the entire Glenn Miller Orchestra, a number of other musical organizations and events, and a presentation by Alan Cass, noted Miller historian. You can reach the society at P.O. Box 61, Clarinda, Iowa, 51632.

Attention Musicians

If you are a musician who likes to travel and would like to perform with the Glenn Miller Orchestra, please send your resume and a performance tape to **Road Manager** at:

**Glenn Miller Productions, Inc.
605 Crescent Executive Court, Suite 300
Lake Mary, FL 32746**

www.glennmillerorchestra.com

ACKNOWLEDGMENTS

This book is crammed with facts and figures and dates obtained from interviews with myriad personnel involved in one way or another with the Glenn Miller Orchestra, and otherwise obtained from various publications of the past, and since.

A book cannot be accomplished by any one person, no matter whose name appears as author. There exists valuable contributions from individuals, so we begin by acknowledging these individuals.

First, the lovely, talented, amazing and gracious **Kathryn Crosby**, who appreciates everyone she meets, as she passionately circumvents the earth to recall to all who will listen, the memory of the great works of her husband **Bing Crosby**. You may find her just about anywhere and everywhere in this honorable quest.

Then, to long time penpal, the great **Patty Andrews** of the legendary Andrews Sisters, always offering good advice and whose memory of the great days she shares so unselfishly. **Jerry Vale**, always anxious to contribute and lend his knowledge and support where it is needed.

To **Larry O'Brien**, a friend for many years, who maintains his enthusiasm for the music and the players and their future, for his unselfish contributions; **Jack Ellsworth**, who, for over 50 years, spins the music we all need to hear on his daily 10-12 AM show on Long Island's WALK radio, "Memories in Melody," always including a Glenn gem recorded at a remote location like the Glen Island Casino or the Hotel Pennsylvania's Cafe Rouge, and a daily, early Bing recording, as well; **Al Monroe**, a Vice President of New York's Chapter of the Society of Singers, and radio personality, who lends his expertise that includes research and provides CDs for all my past and present print efforts; **John Tumpak**, a true expert of big bands history and their musicians, who regularly writes in-depth articles in California jazz magazines, for the use of some of his material; **Jerry Fletcher**, premier Big Band record collector and expert of Florida, who unselfishly verifies facts and figures, and supplies old tapes of interviews for my Big Band chronicles; Big Band leader **Ben Grisafi**, more like a brother then friend, who supplies all he can, tangible and intangible, mostly from the heart; **Dr.Chris Valenti**, of radio WHPC Garden City, New York whose enthusiasm and the sharing of material for interviews and knowledge, is so much appreciated; **Wynne Miller**, who is always enthusiastic and shares her own memories of her Uncle, Glenn Miller; and lovely **Beryl Davis**, Glenn's last vocalist. We have always worked together on many such projects. Anthony DeFlorio III for his unending assistance for all these years.

Max Wirz, of Radio Eviva in Switzerland, whom this book cannot exist without, and whose extensive efforts greatly enhance its quality; big band writer and reviewer, Pennsylvanian **Jack Lebo**, who knows more than I do about all these subjects, but tells the world that I know more than he does; **David Mackay, Jr.**, who encouraged this book from its inception and whose vision and effort keeps the World Famous Glenn Miller Orchestra in continual business every day of the year ever since his dad began it all in 1956. I cannot forget the great and 90 years young Frankie Laine, my original mentor who wrote the foreword for my first book and whom I also regard as a true friend; legendary **Connie Haines**, the bravest and hardest working big band singer who ever lived, whose voice still evokes the magic of the Big Band Era. To me Connie Haines and Helen Forrest were the best singers of that time.

Personal friends **Jerry and Michelle Castleman, Bob Incagliato, Kerry Nix**, and my son **Robert**, my daily expert and assistant in all aspects of these endeavors, John Strano who provided artwork, and, my wife **Madeline**, who contributes her multi talents in preparing this book including designing the cover, and who enthusiastically encourages future endeavors for us to embark upon.

And, my friend **Joe Pardee**, whom we sadly lost just a few months ago. Joe was always there for me providing so much help that it can't be measured in time, content or value. This book is dedicated to him. Besides his family, Joe's first love was the Big Band of Harry James, but was also an admirer of Glenn Miller.

Bob Incagliato

Madeline Grudens

Ben Grisafi

Al Monroe

Robert DeBeltta

Richard Grudens and Kathryn Crosby

Jerry and Michelle
Castleman

Jack Lebo

Jerry Fletcher

Dedication

This book is dedicated to my colleagues:
Joe Pardee and C. Camille Smith

Joe Pardee and I had never met, but his influence on the body of my books has been undeniably overwhelming. I don't know how many recordings of all the music greats were contained in the music library of his home in Fords, New Jersey, but it must have been vast. Joe Pardee was America's representative for the England based Harry James Society. He was a great fan of "Harry," as he endearingly called him, and always attended annual meetings in London with his counterparts.

When I embarked upon writing the life story of Jerry Vale, Joe produced, for my use, every single recording Jerry had ever made. Even Jerry was surprised. When the book was about Bing Crosby, Joe provided almost every recording Bing had ever made, and Joe sent those recordings to me in usable formats: Bing and the Andrews Sisters, or Bing and his movies, or Bing and John Scott Trotter, or Bing's Hawaiian, or Bing with others, and in any other requested format. For this book about Glenn Miller, Joe found endless albums with those ever-precious liner notes and important information about the legendary orchestra leader.

If there is any validity to my books about the big bands, their singers, musicians, arrangers and managers, then I must praise Joe Pardee for his unselfish efforts on behalf of them all and the chronicles that showcase their lives and careers.

Camille Smith was my original photographer. Before he was a colleague, we had been friends. When I discovered his former talent, I enlisted him as my photographer and mentor. He moved a reticent me along at the various venues and provided so many great photos of music people: Dizzy Gillespie, Bob Hope, Ray Anthony, Tony Bennett, Larry O'Brien, Billy Eckstine, Ann Jillian, Rosemary Clooney, Lionel Hampton, Benny Goodman, Margaret Whiting, Frankie Laine, Fran Warren, Helen O'Connell, Eddy Arnold, Herschel Bernardi, Buddy Rich and others. His self-assurance and professionalism was of the highest quality and character.

All of his subjects responded favorably, granting him license to photograph them the way he percieved. In one half hour alone, Camille snapped 85 photos of Bob Hope while I spoke with him. Bob didn't even notice. Camille was my teacher of many things including the art of patience and boldness, and most of all, spirit. He was a great photographer and a true friend.

Glenn Miller Top Tunes Year by Year

The list comprises my personal choice of the best Glenn Miller recordings from 1939 into 1943, although some recordings were produced earlier and released accordingly. This is only a partial list of all Glenn's recordings. This list is not rated, and is strictly my own opinion of Glenn's best works.

1939 Sunrise Serenade - Instrumental
Pavanne - Instrumental
Little Brown Jug - Instrumental
Stairway to the Stars - Ray Eberle
Blue Evening - Ray Eberle
Moonlight Serenade - Instrumental - Theme
My Isle of Golden Dreams - Instrumental
In the Mood - Instrumental
Blue Rain - Ray Eberle
Baby Me - Kay Starr
Love with a Capital You - Kay Starr
Careless - Ray Eberle
1940 Indian Summer - Ray Eberle
Tuxedo Junction - Instrumental
Londonderry Air - Instrumental
The Woodpecker Song - Marion Hutton
Sierra Sue - Ray Eberle
Pennsylvania 6-5000 - Instrumental with Band Chorus
The Nearness of You - Ray Eberle
A Nightingale Sang in Berkeley Square - Ray Eberle
A Handful of Stars - Ray Eberle
Along the Santa Fe Trail - Ray Eberle
1941 Perfidia - Instrumental
Anvil Chorus - Instrumental
Song of the Volga Boatman - Instrumental
You Stepped Out of a Dream - Ray Eberle and the Modernaires
Ida, Sweet as Apple Cider - Tex Beneke
Sweeter Than the Sweetest - Paula Kelly and the Modernaires
Booglie Wooglie Piggy - Paula Kelly, Tex Beneke and the Modernaires
Under Blue Canadian Skies - Ray Eberle
Adios - Instrumental
You and I - Ray Eberle
I Know Why (and So Do You) - Paula Kelly and the Modernaires
I Guess I'll Have to Dream the Rest - Ray Eberle and the Modernaires
Sunrise Serenade - Instrumental
Chattanooga Choo Choo - Tex Beneke, Paula Kelly and the Modernaires
Elmer's Tune - Ray Eberle and the Modernaires
1942 A String of Pearls - Instrumental
Moonlight Cocktail - Instrumental
The White Cliffs of Dover - Ray Eberle
When Johnny Comes Marching Home Again - Tex Beneke, Marion Hutton and
the Modernaires
The Lamplighter's Serenade - Ray Eberle and the Modernaires
Skylark - Ray Eberle
At Last - Ray Eberle
I'm Old Fashioned - Skip Nelson
Kalamazoo - Tex Beneke and the Modernaires
Dearly Beloved - Skip Nelson with Band Chorus
Serenade in Blue - Ray Eberle
Jukebox Saturday Night - Marion Hutton, Tex Beneke and the Modernaires
Moonlight Becomes You - Skip Nelson
1943 That Old Black Magic - Skip Nelson

BIBLIOGRAPHY

Anderson, Ernest, Editor, *Esquire's Jazz Book.* New York, New York: Esquire Inc., 1947

Belaire, David, *A Guide to the Big Band Era.* Santa Ana, California: Winged Note Press, 1996

Cecil, Chuck, *Memory Maker Radio Interviews.* Various Dates.

Dewey, Donald, *James Stewart, A Biography.* Atlanta, Georgia: Turner Publishing 1996

Eberle, Jan, *The Eberle Named Ray.* Redwood, New York: Cadence Jazz Books, 2002

Ewen, David, *American Songwriters.* New York, New York: H.W. Wilson Company, 1987

Grudens, Richard, *The Best Damn Trumpet Player.* Stonybrook, New York: Celebrity Profiles Publishing, 1996

Grudens, Richard, *Jukebox Saturday Night.* Stonybrook, New York: Celebrity Profiles Publishing, 1999

Kennedy, Don & Williams, Hagen, *Big Band Jump Newsletter.* Atlanta, Georgia: 1990-2003

Kernfeld, Barry, Editor, *The New Grove Dictionary of Jazz.* New York, New York: Grove's Dictionaries of Music, Inc. MacMillan Press Limited, London, England, 1988

Lax, Roger and Smith, Frederick, *The Great Song Thesaurus.* New York, New York: Oxford University Press, 1984.

Miller, Glenn, *Method for Orchestral Arranging.* New York, New York: Mutual Music Society, Inc., 1943

Sanford, Herb, *Tommy and Jimmy: The Dorsey Years.* New Rochelle, New York: Arlington House, 1972

Schuller, Gunther, *The Swing Era.* New York, New York: Oxford University Press. 1989

Sforza, John, *Swing It! The Andrews Sisters Story.* Lexington, Kentucky: University Press of Kentucky. 2000

Simon, George,T ., *Glenn Miller and His Orchestra.* New York, New York: Thomas Y. Crowell Company, 1974

Song Hits Magazine. December 1939, Dunellen, New Jersey: Song Lyrics, Inc., 1939

Tumpak, John, *Paul Tanner-From Skunk Hollow to Glenn Miller to UCLA.* and other newsletters. Los Angeles, California, Magazine article, L.A. Jazz Scene. 1995-2003

Walker, Leo, *The Big Band Almanac, Hollywood.* California: Vinewood Enterprises, Inc., 1978

WNEW, "Where the Melody Lingers on" New York, NY, Nightingale Gordon, 1984

Index

Gould, Morton, 202
Grable, Betty, 171, 196
Grappelli, Stephane, 161
Gray, Glen, 9
Gray, Jerry, 67, 96, 118, 126,
   129, 131-33, 135, 143,
   155-56, 157, 183, 188,
   199, 201
Greger, Max, 232, 244, 248,
   256
Gridley, Chad, 265
Griffith, A.C., 75
Grisafi, Ben, 112, 179, 273,
   275
Grudzinski, Richard, 129
Guerra, Freddy, 66
Hackett, Bobby, 2, 29, 36,
   126, 132-33, 138
Haines, Connie, 2, 161-63,
   171-72, 179-80, 270, 274
Hall, Ashley, 265
Hall, Larry, 66
Halliburton, John, 66
Hampton, Lionel, 6, 276
Handy, W.C., 201
Harris, Stanley, 66
Harrison, Mike, 265
Hawkins, Erskine, 104, 200
Hayes, Edgar, 198, 199
Haymes, Dick, 168, 173, 267
Haymes, Joe, 53, 113
Heath, Ted, 161, 221, 236,
   240
Hefti, Neal, 98
Heidt, Horace, 173
Hekkenberg, Mariske, 231
Henderson, Jimmy, 190-91
Henie, Sonja, 18, 205
Herbert, Victor, 202
Herman, Dave, 66
Herman, Woody, 2, 9, 27, 77,
   105, 154, 190
Hilscher, Bill, 268
Hilscher, Nick, 167, 266-69
Holiday, Billie, 269
Hope, Bob, 4, 7, 22, 81, 162-
   63, 276
Hucko, Peanuts, 63, 66, 113,
   125, 157, 189, 220, 223,
   225
Hurok, Sol, 175
Hutton, Betty, 141
Hutton, Marion, 2, 86, 98,
   135, 141, 143, 148, 209
Ippolito, Frank, 67
James, Harry, 3, 6, 25, 42,
   109, 111, 156, 170-73, 196,
   208, 225, 234, 244, 249,
   252-53, 274, 276
Jenney, Brad, 36
Johns, Matt, 167, 265, 266

Joy, Jimmy, 24
Judis, Bernice, 38
Jurgens, Dick, 200
Kane, Murray, 67
Kapp, Jack, 154
Kaproff, Nathan, 66
Kardos, Ernest, 66
Katzman, Harry, 66
Kaye, Danny, 215
Kaye, Sammy, 173, 178, 208
Keene, Linda, 36, 144
Kelly, Paula, 87, 135-37, 144,
   165, 167
Kincaide, Deane, 186
King, Steve, 255
King, Wayne, 173
Klink, Al, 51, 115
Knowles, Legh, 115, 118-19
Kost, Doug, 266
Kowalewski, Joseph, 66
Krupa, Gene, 6, 87, 104-5,
   125, 168, 188, 212
Kuhn, Paul, 223, 232, 244,
   247-48
Kyser, Kay, 163
Laine, Frankie, 139, 274, 276
Lawford, Peter, 212
Lawrence, Jack, 200
Lawrence, Syd, 161, 221,
   236, 240, 252, 255
Lebo, Jack, 274-75
Lee, Peggy, 139
Leeds, Milton, 201
Leinhard, Pepe, 247
Lewis, Joe E., 201
Leyden, Norman, 67
Lipkins, Steve, 36
Lombardo, Guy, 173, 218
Lowe, Mundell, 186
Lund, Art 197
Lynn, Dame Vera, 201
MacGregor, Chummy, 31, 36,
   101, 104, 106, 114, 116,
   132, 181, 198, 212, 214
Mackay, David, Jr., 178, 230,
   274
Mackay, David, Sr., 183
Malvin, Artie 63, 67, 247
Mancini, Henry, 98, 260
Manning, Irene, 247
Marko, Shawn, 266
Marshall, Jerry, 41, 42
Marterie, Ralph, 178
Martin, Freddy, 7
Martin, Skip, 36, 126-27, 159
Maschwitz, Eric, 201
Mastren, Al, 36
Mastren, Carmen, 66, 157
May, Billy, 2, 36, 51, 110,
   129, 131, 133-34, 138-40,
   167, 182, 210, 231, 236,

240, 252
McCoy, Clyde, 39
McIntyre, Hal, 30-31, 36, 51,
   101, 116, 181, 191
McKinley, Ray, 63, 66, 124,
   157, 178, 183-87, 201,
   247, 258
McMickle, Mickey, 36
McPartland, Jimmy, 25
McVay, Ray, 81, 163, 216,
   220, 22-23, 234, 236-39
Meacham, F.W., 199
Mercer, Johnny, 89, 200
Merrick, David, 195
Miller, Deane, 17, 227
Miller, Helen, 26, 27, 79, 106,
   181, 183, 186, 212-13
Miller, Herb, 217, 220, 223,
   225-26
Miller, Irene, 19, 23, 225
Miller, John, 189, 223, 225-
   27, 239
Miller, Lewis Elmer, 45
Miller, Mattie Lou, 22
Miller, Wynne, 2, 16-17, 227,
   274
Mills Brothers, 270
Mince, Johnny, 2, 29, 52-54,
   283
Modernaires, The, 33, 39,
   63, 87, 89, 93, 98, 136,
   143, 159, 165-67, 171,
   182, 206, 212, 246, 250,
   253, 266
Monroe, Al, 273, 275
Monroe, Marilyn, 7
Monroe, Vaughn, 174
Montgomery, George, 209
Mooney, Art, 178
Moonlight Serenaders, The,
   155, 167, 232-33, 238,
   253, 255, 266
Morgan, Harry, 114, 212
Morgan, Johnny, 70
Morgan, Russ, 104, 105
Morrow, Buddy, 3, 178,
   189-90
Morton, Jelly Roll, 198
Motylinski, Richard 66
Moyer, Holly, 23-24
Mucci, Louis, 36
Nash, Dick, 213
Nelson, Ozzie, 139
Nelson, Skip, 159
Nevala, Andy, 266
Nicholas Brothers, 204-5, 206
Nichols, Bobby, 66
Nichols, Loring (Red), 25
Noble, Ray, 28-29, 52, 53,
   127, 140, 185
Norvo, Red, 113

EIGHT GREAT BOOKS

By Richard Grudens

Explore the Golden Age of Music when the Big Bands and their vocalists reigned on the radio and all the great stages of America.

Bing Crosby - Crooner of the Century:
Here is the quintessential Bing Crosby tribute, documenting the story of Crosby's colorful life, family, recordings, radio and television shows, and films; the amazing success story of a wondrous career that pioneered popular music spanning generations and inspiring countless followers.

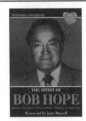

The Spirit of Bob Hope:
Tracing Bob's charmed life from his early days in Cleveland to his worldwide fame earned in vaudeville, radio, television and films and his famous wartime travels for the USO unselfishly entertaining our troops. The best Bob Hope book with testimonials from his friends and a foreword by Jane Russell.

Jerry Vale - A Singer's Life:
The wondrous story of Jerry's life as a kid from teeming Bronx streets of the 1940s to his legendary appearances in the great theatrical venues of America and his three triumphant Carnegie Hall concerts, with appearances at New York's Copacabana, whose magnifi-cent voice has beautifully interpreted the 20th Century's most beautiful love songs.

Snootie Little Cutie:
The story of big band singer, Connie Haines, who sang shoulder to shoulder with Frank Sinatra in the bands of Harry James and Tommy Dorsey, and for years on the Abbott & Costello radio show, and who is still singing today.

www.RichardGrudens.com
EIGHT GREAT BOOKS
By Richard Grudens

Explore the Golden Age of Music when the Big Bands and their
vocalists reigned on the radio and all the great stages of America.

Jukebox Saturday Night:
The final book in the series: interviews with Artie
Shaw, Les Brown and Doris Day, Red Norvo,
Les Paul, Carmel Quinn, stories about Glenn
Miller and the Dorsey Brothers, songwriters
Ervin Drake ("I Believe," "It was a Very Good
Year,") and Jack Lawrence ("Linda," "Tenderly,")
and a special about all the European Bands past
and present.

The Music Men:
A companion to "The Song Stars," about the
great men singers with foreword by Bob Hope;
interviews with Tony Martin, Don Cornell, Julius
LaRosa, Jerry Vale, Joe Williams, Johnny
Mathis, Al Martino, Guy Mitchell, Tex Beneke
and others.

The Song Stars:
A neat book about all the girl singers of the Big
Band Era and beyond: Doris Day, Helen Forrest,
Kitty Kallen, Rosemary Clooney, Jo Stafford,
Connie Haines, Teresa Brewer, Patti Page and
Helen O'Connell and many more.

The Best Damn Trumpet Player:
Memories of the Big Band Era, interviews with
Benny Goodman, Harry James, Woody Herman,
Tony Bennett, Buddy Rich, Sarah Vaughan,
Lionel Hampton, Frankie Laine, Patty Andrews
and others.

Order Books On-line at:

WWW.RICHARDGRUDENS.COM

You Can Fax or Call Your Order In:

Celebrity Profiles Publishing
Box 344, Stonybrook, NY 11790
Ph: (631) 862-8555   Fax (631) 862-0139   Email: celebpro4@aol.com

Title	Price	Pages/ Photos	Qty
The Best Damn Trumpet Player ISBN - 1-57579-011-4	$15.95	196/55	
The Song Stars ISBN - 1-57579-045-9	$17.95	240/60	
The Music Men ISBN - 1-57579-097-1	$17.95	250/70	
Jukebox Saturday Night ISBN - 1-57579-142-0	$17.95	250/70	
Snootie Little Cutie ISBN - 1-57579-143-9	$17.95	144/77	
Jerry Vale - A Singer's Life ISBN - 1-57579-227-3	$19.95	216/117	
The Spirit of Bob Hope **One Hundred Years, One Million Laughs** ISBN - 1-57579-227-3	$19.95	208/132	
Bing Crosby **Crooner of the Century** ISBN - 1-57579-248-6	$19.95	272/171	
Chattanooga Choo Choo **The Life and Times of the World Famous** **Glenn Miller Orchestra** ISBN - 1-57579-277-X	$19.95	296/160	

Name:			
Address:			
City:	State:	Zip:	

Include $3.50 for Priority Mail (2 days arrival time) for up to 2 books. Enclose check or money order. Order will be shipped immediately.

For Credit Cards, please fill out as shown below:

Card #

Exp. Date:

Signature

Card Type (Please Circle):   Visa - Amex - Discover - Master Card